CORDIALS FROM YOUR KITCHEN

Pattie Vargas and Rich Gulling

A Storey Publishing Book

Storey Communications, Inc.
Pownal, Vermont 05261

For Kirsten, Trey, and Nicholas
for their patience and understanding.

*The mission of Storey Communications is to serve our customers
by publishing practical information that encourages
personal independence in harmony with the environment.*

Edited by **Pamela Lappies**
Cover design by **Leslie Morris Noyes and Erin Lincourt**
Cover photograph by **A. Blake Gardner**
Text design by **Cindy McFarland**
Production by **Sarah Crone and Erin Lincourt**
Wood cuts by **Charles Joslin**
Line drawings by **Brigita Fuhrmann**
Indexed by **Northwind Editorial Services**

Copyright © 1997 by Pattie Lee Vargas and Richard Dale Gulling Jr.

The information in this book is true and complete to the best of our knowledge. All recommendations are made without guarantee on the part of the authors or Storey Communications, Inc. The authors and publisher disclaim any liability in connection with the use of this information. For additional information please contact Storey Communications, Inc., Schoolhouse Road, Pownal, Vermont 05261.

Storey Publishing books are available for special premium and promotional uses and for customized editions. For further information, please call the Custom Publishing Department at 1-800-793-9396.

Printed in the United States by R. R. Donnelley
10 9 8 7 6 5 4 3 2 1

Library of Congress Cataloging-in-Publication Data

Vargas, Pattie –
    Cordials from your kitchen : easy, elegant liqueurs you can make / by Pattie Vargas and Rich Gulling.
        p.   cm.
        "A Storey Publishing Book"
        Includes index.
        ISBN 0-88266-986-9 (pbk. : alk. paper) – ISBN 1-58017-019-6 (hc. : alk. paper)
        1. Liqueurs.   I. Gulling, Rich, 1961– .   II. Title.
TP611.V37   1997
641.2'55—dc21   97-14319
                                                              CIP

Contents

INTRODUCTION

When we wrote *Country Wines,* our first book on homemade spirits, our goal was to share the fun of making them with folks who thought the process was difficult and mysterious. Judging from the response, we succeeded quite well.

But the urge to try something new is ever present in our respective kitchens, and a gift of homemade Irish Cream inspired us to try our hands at making liqueurs. What fun!

Homemade liqueurs have many of the advantages of homemade wines. They can be tailored to your taste, the variations are almost endless, they satisfy your creative urge, they make wonderful gifts, and they are scrumptious additions to a variety of foods.

Liqueurs, or cordials, as they are often called, are easier to make and much less expensive than their commercial counterparts. They also are curiously complementary to the fast-paced society in which we live. Even if you start in December, you can make many of the delicious cordials in this book in time for Christmas. Although cordials do require aging, the time needed to make them mellow and delicious is short. Cordials require no special treatment or unusual equipment, and success is ensured if you follow the recipes.

Since you won't be distilling the alcohol for your cordials and will have paid the alcohol tax when you bought it, you won't risk running afoul of the Bureau of Alcohol, Tobacco, and Firearms. As long as you don't sell your creations, you can experiment to your heart's — and taste buds' — content.

A few of the recipes in this book are our attempts at re-creating the flavors of some well-known cordials. Most, however, are our own creations, refined from numerous experiments following a great deal of research. We hope that you enjoy these recipes as much as we enjoyed developing them, and our friends enjoyed sampling them. We also hope that you'll experiment with your own recipes, feel free to vary ours, and, most of all, have fun.

CHAPTER 1

GETTING STARTED

D istilled liquors are the sophisticated cousins of wines, but just as no one is sure who discovered the process of wine making, no one knows for sure who discovered and named the process of distillation. Some credit Hippocrates in about 400 B.C. We do know that the term *distillation* comes from the Latin word *distillare,* which means "to drop" or "to trickle down."

We also know why the process works. Alcohol and water boil at different temperatures. Using this principle, a distiller can heat wine to the temperature at which ethyl alcohol boils (173°F), and the alcohol will turn to vapor. If the distiller then captures the vapor and cools it below 173°F, it will condense into liquid alcohol.

Most experts believe that the Chinese distilled alcohol from rice wine as early as 800 B.C. The Greeks and Egyptians also used distillation, and in about 400 B.C., Aristotle wrote on distilling seawater and recapturing fresh water from the process. The first recorded instance of making alcoholic beverages through distillation dates to A.D. 900, when monks and alchemists in Europe employed the process and experimented with numerous ways of using the fiery liquid that resulted.

During the thirteenth and fourteenth centuries, physicians and chemists believed that herb liqueurs could treat and prevent illnesses. In some cases, they may have been correct, since many modern-day medicines are based on plant extracts and some still have alcohol bases. Even if the mixtures weren't medicinal, those who drank them probably felt better, if only for a short time. Adding sweeteners to the mixtures may have been an attempt by herbalists to make their brews more palatable.

In that, they surely succeeded. Adding other flavoring agents was a logical next step. Liqueur making flourished in fifteenth-

Liqueur or Cordial?

In Europe, alcoholic beverages with a high sugar content and flavoring agents consisting of herbs, nuts, fruits, spices, and creams are called liqueurs. In the United States, these beverages are usually called cordials.

The legal definition of a cordial varies somewhat according to location. New York and New Jersey, for example, defines it as an alcoholic beverage containing at least 2.5 percent sugar.

century Italy in the villas of Catherine de Médici, then spread to France and England. Many of today's liqueurs trace their lineage to those times. Today, as in the past, some of these recipes remain closely guarded secrets, especially those for some herb liqueurs, which may contain dozens or even scores of different herbs in varying proportions. But don't be daunted by liqueur making's long tradition. You can make some very simple and tasty recipes at first, then get more daring as you gain experience.

Choosing Ingredients

Your shopping list for liqueur ingredients can be relatively short or long and complex, but most cordial ingredients fall into definite categories — alcohol bases, sweeteners, and flavorings. As long as your liqueurs have something from each category you will end up with an acceptable cordial. Let's look at these one at a time.

Alcohol Bases

Most cordials range from 17 to 30 percent alcohol by volume, but some have as much as 50 percent. For that reason, the alcohol base you choose is important. Remember that good-quality ingredients result in good-quality liqueurs. Don't buy the cheapest liquors to use in your liqueurs, but you don't need to buy the most expensive either. Since the other ingredients will be the liqueurs' primary flavoring components, some of the subtleties of expensive liquors will be masked anyway. Choose a low- to mid-priced liquor and taste it. If it is free of off flavors — tastes that are non-standard for a particular liquor — or flavors you just don't like, it will be suitable for making liqueurs.

Although most liqueurs are made from grain alcohol, vodka, brandy, and rum, almost any kind of liquor can be used. Here, in order of preference, are some possibilities.

Pure Grain Alcohol: Pure grain alcohol is our choice for making many liqueurs because it has no flavoring components. It is most frequently found in 180- to 190-proof varieties. Because it is a very high proof alcohol, pure grain alcohol is not available in all states and is not legally available in Canada. People who live on the Ohio side of the Ohio-Indiana border, for example, cannot buy high-proof grain alcohol in their state. Those who live on the Indiana side can. Pure grain alcohol is neutral and is usually diluted with an equal part of water in our recipes. All pure grain alcohols are created equal when it comes to making liqueurs. They supply the alcohol component but impart no flavor of their own.

Vodka: Since we live on the Ohio side of the Ohio-Indiana border, we usually use vodka in our liqueur recipes. Like pure grain alcohol, good vodka has little flavor of its own. Vodka can, however, vary in taste from distiller to distiller, so sample it before using. You are looking for the smoothest-tasting vodka in your price range. Pure grain alcohol and vodka are the only bases that will add little flavor to your liqueurs. If your objective is to retain the pure flavors of the fruits, nuts, herbs, spices, and sugars in your recipes, use one of these two bases.

By law, nonflavored vodka that is manufactured in the United States is required to be colorless, odorless, and tasteless. Since that is not always the case with vodkas manufactured elsewhere, we recommend using U.S. varieties.

Brandy: Brandy is distilled from fermented grape juice or the juice of other fruits such as apricots, peaches, and pears. We don't use brandies from fruits other than grapes because they are usually more expensive, and we can make our own flavored brandies more economically. Pick a mid-priced brandy and taste it before using it in your liqueurs. Brandy is not for everyone. A friend of ours once commented that she liked the idea of brandy much more than she liked the taste. She was, however, quite enthusiastic about some of the brandy-based liqueurs presented in this book. If you are not sure if you will like a particular recipe, cut it in half and sample it before you commit yourself to a full batch.

Whiskey: Whiskey is not a common component of liqueurs, although some all-time favorites, such as Bailey's Irish Cream, do have a whiskey base. Some other liqueurs made with whiskey bases are Southern Comfort, Drambuie, Lochan Ora, Glen Mist, and Rock and Rye. Irish and Scotch whiskeys are usually made from malted barley, while American whiskeys are generally distilled from rye, wheat, or corn. The different ingredients result in a considerable variation in taste. If you want to try your hand at making liqueurs from whiskey, pick one whose taste pleases you.

Rum: Few well-known cordials have a rum base, although our rum-based liqueurs were universally popular among our tasters. If you would like to surprise your guests with something unusual,

Cognac

Cognac is a very fine French brandy. Connoisseurs would pale at the thought of using it in liqueurs, but we have used it on occasion. Unless money is no object, however, you'll probably not want to use cognac in your liqueurs.

try one of the rum-based recipes in this book. We think rum and tropical fruits and rum and spices are marriages made in heaven.

Rum is generally distilled from sugar and molasses, so most brands come from the tropical countries where sugarcane is readily available. Rums from Puerto Rico, Barbados, and Costa Rica are usually light bodied and light colored. Jamaican rums are heavier and somewhat sweeter. In some recipes we've specified light or dark rum. In others, it's a matter of personal taste.

Gin: Gin is flavored with juniper berries. Few other ingredients can stand up to juniper berries' strong flavor. For that reason, there are few gin liqueurs and none that proved itself to our tasters. If you try your hand at gin-based liqueurs, you'll have the best luck with citrus-flavored liqueurs, but even here we think a vodka base works better.

Sugars and Other Sweeteners

Liqueurs are sweet drinks. The commonly accepted definition of a liqueur is an alcoholic beverage that contains at least 2.5 percent sugar by weight, but most liqueurs have a much higher sugar content. In fact, a liqueur that contains only 2.5 percent sweetener is considered very dry, and any liqueur with less than 10 percent sweetener can be legally labeled "dry."

The kind of sweetener you choose will affect the flavor of your cordials, so you may want to experiment with various ones. We do not recommend artificial sweeteners, but there are a variety of choices among natural sweetening agents. Most liqueurs are sweet-

Simple Syrup

Combine equal parts sugar and water in a saucepan. Bring the mixture to a boil over medium-high heat, stirring constantly until the sugar dissolves. Don't boil the mixture for a long period of time. Once the mixture is clear, remove from heat.

ened with ordinary table sugar (sucrose). Because sugar is more soluble in water than it is in alcohol, we make the blending process easier by using a "simple syrup" to sweeten our cordials. Simple syrup is made by heating sugar and water in equal parts until a clear, liquid syrup forms.

As we experimented with various recipes for cordials, we realized that some liqueurs taste better when made with other sweeteners such as brown sugar, honey, and corn syrup. All of these sweeteners are acceptable, but simple syrup is our choice for most of the liqueurs because it doesn't impart a distinctive flavor of its own. A few of our recipes call for flavored syrup in addition to simple syrup. These are among the easiest recipes in the book.

Sweeteners help give liqueurs their characteristic body, but sometimes by themselves they cannot create the body texture, or "mouth feel," that most people associate with liqueurs. That's why some of the recipes call for glycerin, an odorless, colorless liquid made from hydrolized fats or oils. It gives cordials a more full-bodied texture and has a slight preservative action. Using glycerin in any recipe is optional.

Water

You can use tap water in making liqueurs if it is relatively free of minerals. Most public water systems have removed some of the mineral content from water, but we've noticed that some well water in our area has a heavy iron and calcium content that may change the flavor of a liqueur. If you are worried about the taste these mineral salts might impart, use bottled or distilled water to make simple syrup. If minerals are not a problem, using tap water will be fine even if it is chlorinated. Heating the water will cause any chlorine in the water to evaporate, and the flavor it imparts will disappear.

Flavorings

Liqueurs take their flavors from a wide variety of fruits, nuts, and spices, as well as coffees, teas, and cream. The ways to use these flavoring agents vary. We'll tell you more about this later, but first let's look at some of the flavoring possibilities. The chart on the next two pages lists favorite flavorings for liqueurs.

Common Flavorings for Liqueurs

Flavor	Form	Source Location
Almond (bitter)	Apricot kernels	France, California
Angelica	Root	Belgium
Aniseed	Seed	Spain, Morocco, Italy, Mexico
Apple	Fruit	Various
Apricot	Fruit	Various
Artemisia	Leaf, flower	Asia, South America
Banana	Fruit, peel	Central America
Bilberry	Fruit	Central Europe
Blackberry	Fruit	Various
Black currant	Fruit	Europe
Blueberry	Fruit	United States
Caraway	Seed	Holland, Poland
Cardamom	Seedpod, seeds	India, Sri Lanka, Guatemala
Cherry	Fruit, pit	Various
Cinchona	Bark	South America, Java
Cinnamon	Bark	Sri Lanka
Clove	Flower	Madagascar
Cocoa	Bean	Venezuela, Ivory Coast
Coconut	Flesh	Various
Coffee	Bean	Various
Coriander	Seed	Morocco
Cranberry	Fruit	United States, Finland
Cumin	Seed	North Africa
Dill	Seed	Various
Elderberry	Fruit, flower	United States
Fennel	Seed	France, Italy
Ginger	Root	Jamaica, Nigeria
Ginseng	Root	China
Grapefruit	Fruit, peel	Various
Hazelnut	Nut	United States
Hyssop	Leaf	Southern Europe
Juniper	Berry	Various

Flavor	Form	Source Location
Lemon	Peel	Various
Licorice	Root	Mediterranean region
Macadamia nut	Kernel	Hawaii
Mace	Nutmeg peel	East Indies
Maidenhair	Fern	Central and South America
Mandarin orange	Peel	Algeria, South Africa
Mint	Leaf	Various
Myrrh	Resin	East Africa, Arabia
Nutmeg	Kernel	East Indies
Orange	Peel	Various
Orange (bitter)	Peel	Various
Orris	Root	Italy
Peach	Fruit	Various
Pear	Fruit	Various
Pimento	Berry	Jamaica
Pineapple	Fruit	Hawaii
Pine nut	Seed	Various
Raspberry	Fruit	Various
Rose	Flower, fruit	Various
Rosemary	Leaf	Various
Saffron	Flower	Southern Europe, Asia
Sage	Leaf	Europe, United States
Shaddock	Peel	Southern United States
Sloe	Fruit, kernel	France, Hungary
Strawberry	Fruit	United States, Europe
Tea	Leaf	Sri Lanka, India, China
Thyme	Leaf	Various
Vanilla	Seedpod	Madagascar
Verbena	Leaf	Various

Zesting

Most of the flavoring elements in citrus fruits are in the peel. Many of our recipes call for lemon, grapefruit, or orange zest. You can buy a zester at any store that sells specialty kitchen equipment, or you can use a vegetable peeler to remove just the colored outer rind of the fruit. Do not include any of the white inner peel; it has a bitter aftertaste.

Flavors for liqueurs are usually extracted by one of three methods: infusion or maceration, percolation, or distillation. *Infusion* and *maceration* are quite similar and involve steeping crushed fruits, spices, or herbs in either water, called infusion, or alcohol, called maceration. The water or alcohol absorbs most of the flavor and color of the fruit. Most of our recipes use maceration. *Percolation* is sometimes called brewing, and as the name suggests, it is similar to making coffee. In this process, spirits are allowed to trickle through the flavoring agent, such as fruit, spices, or herbs. The process is repeated many times over weeks or months. *Distillation* uses heat to extract flavor and requires special equipment. Since our goal was to make the liqueur-making process as easy as possible and home distillation is illegal, we have not used distillation in any of the recipes in this book.

Fruit-flavored liqueurs take their flavors and colors from the fruits used to make them. To get the maximum flavor from the fruit, the alcohol must come into contact with as much surface area as possible. The easiest way to accomplish this is to crush or finely chop the fruit. In most cases, you can include the peel and even the pit in your mixture. Since crushed fruits tend to clump together when mixed with alcohol and aged for several days or weeks, you'll need to stir or shake the fruit-alcohol mixture as it steeps to ensure maximum flavor.

If you are making liqueurs flavored with spices, we recommend buying fresh ones and grinding them yourself. Ground varieties are expensive and will have lost some of their flavor even before they're opened, since volatile oils that contain most of the flavor start to evaporate rather quickly. A more economical and flavorful solution is to buy spices unground, at a health food store. Use a coffee grinder to grind them just before using them in your recipes.

If you are making nut liqueurs — some of our personal favorites — toasting the nuts in a moderate oven (350°F) for a few minutes before chopping improves their flavor, but you may skip this step and still get delicious nut liqueurs.

All flavoring components are not created equal. In our recipes, we used concentrated extracts and oils — the kinds often used for making candy. You can find sources for these flavorings in the back of this book. They are also sometimes available at gourmet coffee shops and in specialty cooking stores. If you use the less concentrated flavorings found in supermarkets, you may need from two to four times as much as you need if you use concentrated flavorings. We suggest that you add the recommended amount in the recipe, taste, and then adjust according to your preference.

Quick and Easy Cordials

If you are at home in the kitchen and like being there, you might enjoy the process of making your own cordials as much as you enjoy the products. But in our increasingly busy world, time is often short. As we experimented, we found that using flavored syrups, flavoring oils, and extracts greatly reduced the time and energy it took to create delicious cordials. These flavoring agents may contain one or more ingredients. They make the process of creating liqueurs so easy and foolproof that you may find yourself with dozens of different varieties. (See page 161 for a list of manufacturers of these laborsaving oils, extracts, and syrups.) You'll be able to put together a batch of cordials in record time and create a unique and personal hostess gift on the spur of the moment. In this book, we include both standard recipes, which will satisfy those of you who enjoy the process, and some "Quick and Easy" recipes, which will please those who are in a hurry.
Look for the Quick and Easy symbol throughout the book.

QUICK & EASY

Coloring

The alcohol and sugar in fruit-flavored liqueurs usually extract color as well as flavor from the fruit bases, but many liqueurs are also artificially colored. If you make an elderberry liqueur, you won't need to add a coloring agent. But liqueurs made from herbs, spices, and some other flavoring agents may not have the color you have come to associate with that flavor. Orange liqueur, for example, will be largely clear unless you add food coloring to give it the traditional orange color. Since food coloring does not affect flavor, you may add or omit it as you choose.

Cream Bases

Cream-based liqueurs are the aristocrats of the liqueur family. They are rich and flavorful, delicious alone or over ice, and wonderful in coffee or over ice cream. They dress up desserts — or become desserts themselves — for a fitting climax to a grand meal.

Many of the cream liqueur recipes that friends and colleagues gave us called for refrigeration and recommended consumption within a couple of weeks. Yet commercially bottled cream liqueurs, such as Irish cream, have no such restrictions. Theoretically, the alcohol retards spoilage, but we are not willing to take the chance with our cream liqueurs, so we keep them in the refrigerator. We are not sure what the maximum time for storing a cream-based liqueur is. (Ours never last long enough for us to find out.) We have stored them in the refrigerator for more than a month without any ill effects. In fact, the flavors mellow with time.

We recommend, therefore, that you make the cream-based liqueurs in relatively small quantities and use them within two to four weeks. Pay particular attention to cleanliness, and make sure to use sterile equipment.

The Right Equipment

If you have a well-equipped kitchen, you shouldn't need to purchase any special equipment to make liqueurs. Even if you are missing one or two items, you can probably adapt. It is important, however, that all equipment be clean and well rinsed so that you don't get any unwanted residue or off flavors from lingering soap or detergent. Although alcohol is a sterilizing agent at high concentrations, the concentration in your liqueurs may not be high enough to have this effect. Since the liqueurs will be aged and bacteria or yeast could be present, we usually take the precaution of sterilizing the containers we're going to use for aging. You can boil glass or metal containers for 15 minutes to accomplish this task, but we usually just run them through the dishwasher and then through an additional rinse cycle to make sure all detergent residue has been rinsed away. We prefer to use metal or glass utensils, since some plastics may impart off flavors to the liqueurs. Following are some of the items we've found useful:

MEASURING DEVICES
- ❐ Glass 1-quart measuring cup
- ❐ Metal measuring spoons
- ❐ Metal funnel
- ❐ Wooden spoons

STRAINERS AND FILTERING DEVICES
- ❐ Fine-mesh strainer (such as metal tea strainer)
- ❐ Coarse sieve or colander
- ❐ Cloth jelly bag
- ❐ Large coffee filters (for 30-cup coffeemakers)
- ❐ Cheesecloth
- ❐ Three to 4 feet of plastic aquarium tubing (the plastic is neutral and will not impart off flavors)
- ❐ White muslin

AGING CONTAINERS
- ❐ Wide-mouthed glass jars with lids (1-quart or 2-quart size)
- ❐ Wine or liquor bottles with tight-fitting lids
- ❐ Assorted decanters, cruets, and decorative bottles with lids or new corks

A Word about Racking

Not all the cordials in this book require filtering or racking (drawing the liquid off from the solids). Those that use prepared flavoring agents, those with cream bases, and those that have only liquid ingredients may not require any filtering. Other liqueurs may be filtered using cheesecloth, muslin, or coffee filters.

When we began making liqueurs, we put our wine-making experience to use and tried racking rather than filtering. We found that we prefer racking liqueurs for several reasons — racking is less time-consuming and wasteful, and we think it gives better results — but if you are uncomfortable with racking, filtering will work fine. Adding glycerin to a liqueur gives it more body and the "mouth

A Word of Caution

Be very careful about the kinds of bottles you use to store your liqueurs. Many substances are more soluble in alcohol than they are in water. If you reuse storage containers, make sure to use those that have held wine or liquor. Containers that have held things other than food may transfer bad-tasting or even dangerous contaminants to your liqueurs. Don't use plastic water bottles, milk jugs, or soft drink bottles. Avoid old lead crystal decanters or cruets. The lead may leach into your beverages if you store them for a long period of time.

If you're using corks to close your bottles, use new ones. Old or used corks can impart an off taste or crumble from age.

feel" that many people associate with liqueurs, but these thicker liqueurs take longer to filter. When you pour some of the heavier liqueurs through a coffee filter, for example, it takes a long time for the liqueur to filter through because the residue tends to clog the pores of the filter paper. If you use cheesecloth or muslin, the cloth soaks up a lot of the liqueur in addition to filtering out the solids. For that reason, if you do filter your liqueurs, we recommend wetting the filter, cheesecloth, or muslin with water to make it less absorbent.

Racking eliminates both problems. As your liqueurs age, the solids tend to sink to the bottom of the container, leaving the cleared liquid at the top. Racking the liquid into another container leaves the solids that can cloud your liqueur behind.

Racking is really quite simple. You'll need 3 to 4 feet of clear plastic aquarium tubing and a clean container in addition to the one you've used for aging. We usually place the container we're racking *into* in the kitchen sink and set the container we're racking *from* on an overturned saucepan on the countertop. The container that you are racking *from* must be higher than the one that you are racking *into* so that siphoning will work. Any method you use to keep the full container higher than the empty one will work.

Place the tubing in the liqueur, taking care to leave any sediment undisturbed. Start the siphoning action by sucking on the free end of the tube, much as you would on a straw. Be sure that the end of the tube is at least an inch above the sediment on the bottom of the container. When the liquid starts to flow, tuck the end of the tube into the clean container. The liquid will continue to flow downward until it is transferred to the new container, leaving the sediment behind.

Bottling, Storing, and Gift Ideas

You can use any bottle with a tight-fitting lid to store your liqueur once it is filtered or racked. We usually just transfer the liqueur to the bottle that contained the alcohol base. Brandy, for example, often comes with a capped cork, which is attractive as well as practical. Vodka and other liquor bottles usually have reusable screw caps. In addition, wine bottles are easily refitted with new corks. Some people store liqueurs in small containers such as baby food jars. We store our cream-based liqueurs, which are thicker than other liqueurs and require refrigeration, in fruit, or canning, jars.

Most liqueurs, except those made with a cream base, will last indefinitely if you keep them tightly closed. A cork or lid serves two purposes: It keeps the alcohol, which evaporates quickly when exposed to the air, in the bottle, and it keeps dust and other unwanted substances out of the bottle. Store your homemade cordials in a cupboard or with your other liquors where they will improve with age, as the flavors blend and mellow. Even cream-based liqueurs will be smoother after a week or so of refrigeration.

A homemade liqueur creatively packaged can be as satisfying to give as it is to receive. You'll find a number of gift-giving suggestions here and throughout the book to get you started.

♦ Fill clean baby food jars — label removed — with your favorite liqueur. Add your own label (see page 165 for labels). Use pinking shears to cut a circle of fabric about 1½ inches larger than the lid, then put the "bonnet" of fabric over the lid and tie with matching yarn or a strip of grosgrain ribbon.

♦ If your budget is a bit bigger, prepare two or three varieties of the above, and nestle them in a basket lined with the same fabric used to cover the lids.

♦ You can find some lovely bottles in various colors, complete with corks, in your local discount department store and in upscale home furnishing stores. Fill them with hazelnut liqueur, add labels and gold ribbon, and give as Christmas gifts.

♦ Fill a wooden spice rack with flavored liqueurs for an unlikely-to-be-duplicated gift.

♦ Fill the carafe of a wine set or a crystal decanter with liqueur.

♦ Make a cruet filled with liqueur part of a gift basket containing gourmet crackers, cheeses, and fresh fruit. This one makes a great hostess gift.

CHAPTER 2

SOMETHING FRUITY

aking liqueurs from fresh fruit is an especially satisfying way to retain the flavor of the fruit. When we make wine, we know that identical recipes and methods can produce wines with different characters and taste qualities. Wine making is an adventure precisely because the natural processes that result in wine involve an element of chance.

Homemade cordials are more predictable. The alcohol bases for cordials are made by experts. You can control the proof — the amount of alcohol present in the cordials — just by measuring carefully. The amount of sweetener you add will control the sweetness of the final product. The fruit will not need to ferment to flavor the liqueurs, so the final taste will be closer to that of the fruit you use in their preparation. Cordials are also easier to "repair" if you mistakenly add too much or not enough sugar, flavoring, or alcohol.

Homemade fruit-flavored cordials share one important characteristic with homemade wines: You cannot make superior wines or cordials from inferior fruit. Always use ripe, unblemished fruit. Taste the fruit before you use it in a cordial. If the raw fruit doesn't taste good, it won't taste good in the cordial. Just as the fruit's good flavors are intensified in the cordial, its bad ones are, too.

We still make homemade wines, and they are popular with our friends and families, but we get many more requests for our cordial recipes. And sometimes we say no.

Berries are fragile fruits — easily bruised, quick to spoil, and fleeting in their availability. Ripe red raspberries, plump purple elderberries, and blueberries bursting with sweetness owe part of their appeal to their short seasons, which make them a special treat. Canning, freezing, and drying are just a few of the ways berry lovers have tried to prolong their indulgence. We think that it's long past time to add berry cordials to their list of options.

Blackberry Liqueur

Packed with flavor blackberries transform almost any food they touch into a feast. If you are making cordials for the first time, try this recipe. But be warned: You might become so hooked on blackberries that you'll brave bulls, burdock, and poison ivy to bring in a bucketful from the wilds!

- 2 cups fresh blackberries, picked over and washed
- 1 cup sugar
- 1 cup 100-proof vodka
- 1 cup brandy
- 1 cup light corn syrup
- 1 teaspoon lemon zest
- 1 tablespoon fresh-squeezed lemon juice

Place berries in clean 2-quart jar and add sugar. Crush berries with wooden spoon and let stand for 1 hour. Add vodka and brandy, tightly cap, and shake vigorously. Add corn syrup, lemon zest, and lemon juice. Let stand in a cool, dark place for 2 weeks.

Use a fine-mesh strainer to strain out solids. Discard. Transfer liqueur to clean container and let stand for 1 week. Rack or filter into final container. Cover and age for 1 month more before serving. YIELD: APPROX. 1 QUART

Blackberry Liqueur QUICK & EASY

- 1½ cups sugar
- 1 cup water
- 1½ teaspoons concentrated blackberry flavoring extract
- 1½ cups 100-proof vodka

Make a simple syrup by bringing sugar and water to a boil over medium-high heat, stirring constantly to prevent scorching. When clear, remove from heat and let stand until just warm. Pour into clean 1-quart jar with tight-fitting lid. Add flavoring and vodka, cover, and shake well. This cordial may be served immediately, but it's better if allowed to age for 1 month. YIELD: APPROX. 1 FIFTH

Black Currant Liqueur

Currants were never high on our list of fruits we'd yearn for on a desert island. Then we tasted black currant liqueur.

- 1½ pounds black currants, destemmed
- 3 cups 100-proof vodka
- 2 cups sugar
- 1 cup boiling water
- 1 teaspoon lemon zest
- 1 tablespoon fresh-squeezed lemon juice

Using Leftovers

You can freeze leftover currants to add to spice cake or fruitcake. The sediment left by the aging process can be mixed with oil and vinegar to make a marinade for poultry.

Place currants and 1 cup of sugar in a clean 2-quart, wide-mouthed jar. Crush with wooden spoon, then cover with vodka. Cover and let stand in a cool, dark place for 4 days, shaking morning and evening. Strain vodka through fine mesh into clean 2-quart jar, reserving currants in first jar. Pour remaining sugar and water over currants. Cover both jars tightly and let stand for 3 days, shaking twice a day.

Use a fine-mesh strainer to strain currant liquid into saucepan. Bring to a boil over medium-high heat and boil for 3 minutes, then pour over currants. Let stand until just warm. Add strained vodka, lemon zest, and lemon juice. Let stand, covered, for 3 days.

Use a fine-mesh strainer to strain into clean container. Let stand for 1 week before racking or filtering into final container. Age for 2 months more before serving. YIELD: APPROX. 1½ QUARTS

Black Currant Liqueur *QUICK & EASY*

- 1½ cups sugar
- 1 cup water
- 1½ teaspoons concentrated black currant extract
- 1½ cups 100-proof vodka

Make a simple syrup by bringing sugar and water to a boil over medium-high heat, stirring constantly to prevent scorching. When clear, remove from heat and let stand until just warm. Pour into clean 1-quart jar. Add extract and vodka, cover tightly, and shake well. This cordial may be served immediately, but it's better if aged for 1 month. YIELD: APPROX. 1 FIFTH

Containers for Cordials

Although liqueurs can be stored in virtually any container, we think cordials and cruets are a perfect combination. Over the years, we've amassed a large collection of antique cruets in dozens of shapes, sizes, and colors. Cut- or pressed-glass cruets manufactured between 1850 and 1910 often take on a lavender hue when they are exposed to sunlight because the glass from that period has a high manganese content.

Blueberry Liqueur

Part of the appeal of fruit liqueurs is that they come in such a wide variety of beautiful colors. Even if blueberry cordials didn't taste so good — and they most decidedly do — they would be worth making for their color. Serving blueberry cordials from stoppered, cut-glass cruets is a treat for the senses. They look, smell, and taste delightful.

> 2 cups fresh blueberries, picked over and washed
> 1 cup sugar
> 1 cup 100-proof vodka
> ½ cup brandy
> ¾ cup light corn syrup
> 1 teaspoon lemon zest
> 1 tablespoon fresh-squeezed lemon juice

Place berries in a clean 2-quart jar and add sugar. Crush berries with wooden spoon and let stand for 1 hour. Add vodka and brandy, tightly cap, and shake vigorously. Add corn syrup, lemon zest, and lemon juice. Cover and let stand in a cool, dark place for 2 weeks.

Use a fine-mesh strainer to strain out solids. Discard. Transfer liqueur to clean container and let stand for 1 week. Rack or filter into final container. Age for 1 month more before serving.
YIELD: APPROX. 1 QUART

Cranberry Liqueur

If cranberries have always been your least favorite part of the traditional Thanksgiving menu, it might not be a bad idea to treat yourself to this cranberry concoction. You may find that you're instantly thankful that you had your cranberries cordial fashion!

    3 cups fresh cranberries (one 12 ounce bag), picked over and washed
    2 cups sugar
    1 cup water
 1½ cups 100-proof vodka
    2 teaspoons grapefruit zest

Zesty Cranberry

This liqueur is zingy, zesty, and surprisingly refreshing. We tasted it with a little trepidation, but it tastes as good as it looks — and it looks fantastic. It has the clear red color of a good claret and is beautiful served in cut-glass cordial glasses. It also mellows with age. You may want to make extra during cranberry season to last for the entire year.

Coarsely chop cranberries in food processor or blender and transfer to clean 2-quart container. Add sugar, stir, and let stand for 1 hour. Add water, vodka, and grapefruit zest. Cover tightly and let stand in a cool, dark place for 1 month. Shake 2 to 3 times a week to prevent clumping of fruit.

Use a coarse sieve or colander to strain out solids. Discard. Strain again using a fine-mesh strainer. Transfer to clean container and let stand for 1 week. Rack or filter into final container. Cover and age for at least 1 month more before serving.

YIELD: APPROX. 1 QUART

Elderberry Liqueur

In Ohio, where we live, elderberries grow wild along fencerows. Our first taste of them was in homemade elderberry jelly, and it was love at first bite. When we began making cordials, we were more interested in elderberries for their beautiful color than for their taste. We weren't disappointed in that department — this liqueur has the most striking deep purple color of any liqueur we've made — and just wait until you taste it! Sophisticated wine drinkers, occasional drinkers, and inexperienced cordial tasters were unanimous in their praise.

- 4 cups fresh elderberries, picked over and washed
- 2 cups sugar
- 1 teaspoon lemon zest
- 2 tablespoons fresh-squeezed lemon juice
- 1 cup water
- 3 cups 100-proof vodka

Crush elderberries and sugar together in bowl. Let stand for about 1 hour. Add lemon zest and lemon juice. Transfer to clean 2-quart container and add water and vodka. Cover and let stand in a cool, dark place for 1 month, shaking occasionally.

Use a fine-mesh strainer to strain out solids. Discard. Transfer liqueur to clean container and let stand for 1 week. Rack or filter into final container. Cover and age for at least 1 month more before serving. YIELD: APPROX. 1½ QUARTS

Raspberry Liqueur

Raspberry liqueur has everything — wonderful flavor, beautiful color, tempting aroma, and a variety of uses in addition to the supremely satisfying one of simply sipping it from a stemmed cordial glass.

1½	pounds fresh raspberries, picked over and washed
1	cup sugar
3	cups white zinfandel
1½	cups 100-proof vodka
2	cups water

Crush raspberries and sugar together in bowl. Let stand for about 1 hour. Transfer to clean 2-quart container and add zinfandel, vodka, and water. Cover and let stand in a cool, dark place for 3 days, shaking frequently.

Use a fine-mesh strainer to strain out solids. Discard. Transfer liqueur to clean container and let stand for 1 week. Rack or filter into final container. Age for at least 1 month more before serving. YIELD: APPROX. 1½ QUARTS

Holiday Hints

For a jolly holiday season, fill some tiny cordial glasses with raspberry liqueur and others with green mint or pistachio liqueur. Serve with a variety of cheeses, crackers, and dips. Or serve parfaits in tall champagne glasses, with these elegant liqueurs swirled with vanilla ice cream and topped with chocolate curls.

Raspberry Liqueur

1½	cups sugar
1	cup water
1½	teaspoons concentrated raspberry flavoring extract
1½	cups 100-proof vodka

Make a simple syrup by bringing sugar and water to a boil over medium-high heat, stirring constantly to prevent scorching. When clear, remove from heat and let stand until just warm. Pour into clean 1-quart jar with tight-fitting lid. Add flavoring and vodka, cover, and shake well. This cordial may be served immediately, but it's better if allowed to age for 1 month. YIELD: APPROX. 1 FIFTH

Visual Appeal

Hypocras is another cordial that captures the beautiful color of the fresh fruit. Show it off in a clear, distinctive bottle.

Hypocras

This liqueur, adapted from a very old French recipe, is testimony to the age-old desire to preserve the flavor of fresh strawberries for enjoyment year-round. A more modern French liqueur called Liqueur de Fraise is available commercially, but you may find that you prefer your own version, since you can vary the ingredients to suit your taste. Hypocras has just a hint of cinnamon and a blend of wine, brandy, and vodka, which makes it more complex in taste than the strawberry liqueur recipe that follows it.

 2 cups fresh strawberries, stemmed and washed
 2 cups sugar
 3 cups white zinfandel, rosé wine, or
    strawberry wine
 1 cup brandy
 ½ cup 100-proof vodka
 1 tablespoon fruit protector (optional)
 1 teaspoon lemon zest
 1 cinnamon stick

Crush strawberries and sugar together in bowl. Let stand about 1 hour. Transfer to clean 2-quart container and add wine, brandy, vodka, fruit protector (if using), lemon zest, and cinnamon stick. Cover and let stand in a cool, dark place for 3 days, shaking frequently.

Use a fine-mesh strainer to strain out solids. Discard. Transfer liqueur to clean container, cover, and let stand for 1 week. Rack or filter into final container. Cover and age for at least 1 month more before serving. YIELD: APPROX. 2 QUARTS

Scrumptious Strawberry Liqueur

If you were the kid who asked for just plain strawberries when everyone else was having strawberry shortcake or a strawberry sundae, you will instantly understand the appeal of this liqueur. The orange and lemon zests seem to intensify the strawberry flavor.

    3   cups fresh strawberries, stemmed and washed
    1½ cups sugar
    2   cups 100-proof vodka
    1   cup water
    ½   teaspoon lemon zest
    1   teaspoon orange zest
    1   teaspoon fresh-squeezed lemon juice

Crush strawberries and sugar together in bowl. Let stand for about 1 hour. Transfer to clean 2-quart container and add vodka, water, lemon zest, orange zest, and lemon juice. Cover and let stand in a cool, dark place for 2 days, shaking frequently.

Use a fine-mesh strainer to strain out solids. Discard. Transfer liqueur to clean container, cover, and let stand for 1 week. Rack or filter into final container. Age for at least 1 month more before serving. YIELD: APPROX. 1 QUART

Strawberry Liqueur *QUICK & EASY*

    1½ cups sugar
    1   cup water
    1½ teaspoons concentrated strawberry flavoring
        extract
    1½ cups 100-proof vodka

Make a simple syrup by bringing sugar and water to a boil over medium-high heat, stirring constantly to prevent scorching. When clear, remove from heat and let stand until just warm. Pour into clean 1-quart jar with tight-fitting lid. Add flavoring and vodka, cover, and shake well. This cordial may be served immediately, but it's better if allowed to age for 1 month. YIELD: APPROX. 1 FIFTH

Orchard and Garden Fruits

Liqueurs made from orchard and garden fruits are among the most popular "kitchen cordials" on the list of homemade potables. The fruits are inexpensive, readily available, and easy to work with. If you are uncomfortable with more exotic liqueurs, these cordials are great confidence builders. They are almost foolproof and retain the charm of old-time flavors — the kind that remind you of Grandma's kitchen, redolent of lemon tarts and homemade peach pie.

Apple Liqueur

Apple liqueur is the exception to the always-use-ripe-fruit rule. For this recipe, use green apples, which increase the acidity of the cordial, giving it just enough bite to make it interesting.

1 cup white sugar
1 cup dark brown sugar
1½ cups water
2½ pounds fresh green apples, stemmed and washed
1 teaspoon lemon zest
1 cinnamon stick
2 cups 100-proof vodka
1 cup brandy

Make a simple syrup by bringing white sugar, brown sugar, and water to a boil over medium-high heat, stirring constantly to prevent scorching. When clear, remove from heat and let stand until just warm. Quarter and core apples. Slice into clean 2-quart container with tight-fitting lid. Pour syrup over apples and add lemon zest, cinnamon, vodka, and brandy. Cover and let stand in a cool, dark place for about 1 month.

Rack or filter liqueur into final container such as wine botte, fruit jar, or decanter. YIELD: APPROX. 1½ QUARTS

Apple Liqueur

1½ cups sugar
1 cup water
1½ teaspoons concentrated apple flavoring extract
1½ cups 100-proof vodka

Make a simple syrup by bringing sugar and water to a boil over medium-high heat, stirring constantly to prevent scorching. When clear, remove from heat and let stand until just warm. Pour into clean 1-quart jar with tight-fitting lid. Add flavoring and vodka, cover, and shake well. This cordial may be served immediately, but it's better if allowed to age for 1 month. YIELD: APPROX. 1 FIFTH

Dried Apricot Liqueur

We like to use dried apricots to make apricot liqueurs because the drying process concentrates the flavor. This is a lovely golden liqueur with an exquisite taste.

- 1 cup water
- 2 cups sugar
- 1 pound dried apricots, chopped
- ¾ cup 100-proof vodka
- ¾ cup brandy
- 1 teaspoon orange zest
- 1 tablespoon fruit protector
- 5 drops yellow food coloring
- 2 drops red food coloring

Make a simple syrup by bringing sugar and water to a boil over medium-high heat, stirring constantly to prevent scorching. When clear, remove from heat and let stand until just warm. Place apricots in 2-quart jar with tight-fitting lid. Pour syrup over apricots and add vodka, brandy, orange zest, fruit protector, and yellow and red food coloring. Cover and let stand in a cool, dark place for about 1 month.

Rack or filter liqueur into final container such as wine bottle, fruit jar, or decanter. YIELD: APPROX. 1 QUART

Apricot Liqueurs

Apricot liqueurs are delicious straight up or on the rocks. They're also rich and mellow mixed with half-and-half and served over ice. Roasted pork, chicken, and ham are doubly delicious glazed with a mixture of apricot liqueur, teriyaki sauce, and a hint of cinnamon.

Ideas for Apricots

You may use the macerated apricots as an exotic addition to stuffing for roast chicken or turkey — and don't forget to use the liqueur as a delicious glaze for the bird.

Fruit Protector

Fruit protector lends acidity to liqueurs, resulting in improved taste. It is used in recipes calling for fresh or dried fruit, and sometimes when there is no fruit at all!

Honey-Apricot Liqueur

This mellow liqueur rolls over your tongue like pure, golden nectar. Use only apricots that are completely ripe and unblemished to make this cordial.

4–6 fresh, ripe apricots, stemmed and washed
1 tablespoon fresh-squeezed lemon juice
1 cup honey
1 cup dry white wine
1 cup 100-proof vodka
½ cup brandy
1 teaspoon orange zest
1 teaspoon pure vanilla extract

Cut apricots in half, remove pits, and quarter. Place in clean 2-quart jar and sprinkle with lemon juice. Bring honey and wine to a boil over medium-high heat. Boil for 2 to 3 minutes, skimming off any foam. Pour the liquid over the apricots and let stand until just warm. Add vodka, brandy, orange zest, and vanilla. Cover and let stand in a cool, dark place for 3 weeks, shaking 2 to 3 times per week.

Use coarse sieve or colander to strain out solids. Discard. Strain the liquid through fine mesh into clean container; let stand for 1 week, covered. Rack or filter into final container. Cap and age for 1 month more before serving. YIELD: APPROX. 1 QUART

Apricot Liqueur

1½ cups sugar
1 cup water
1½ teaspoons concentrated apricot flavoring extract
1½ cups 100-proof vodka

Make a simple syrup by bringing sugar and water to a boil over medium-high heat, stirring constantly to prevent scorching. When clear, remove from heat and let stand until just warm. Pour into clean 1-quart jar. Add flavoring and vodka, cover tightly, and shake well. Cordial may be served immediately, but it's better if aged for 1 month. YIELD: APPROX. 1 FIFTH

Cherry Liqueur

Cherry fans will love this cordial. It's pretty, piquant, and practically foolproof. Make it with pie cherries for a light-colored liqueur, or use dark Bing cherries for a darker, mellower cordial. We're willing to bet that whichever one you choose, you'll want to try the other variety, too, as soon as you take your first taste. This liqueur is particularly nice served in stemmed cordial glasses so that you can enjoy the beautiful color.

> 2 cups sugar
> 1 cup water
> 1½ pounds fresh cherries with pits, stemmed and
>   washed
> 2½ cups 100-proof vodka
> 1 cup brandy
> 1 teaspoon lemon zest
> 1 tablespoon fruit protector

Make a simple syrup by bringing sugar and water to a boil over medium-high heat, stirring constantly to prevent scorching. When clear, remove from heat and let stand until just warm. Cut cherries in half but don't remove pits. Put cherries and pits in clean 2-quart container with tight-fitting lid. Pour syrup over cherries and add vodka, brandy, lemon zest, and fruit protector. Cover and let stand in a cool, dark place for 2 weeks, shaking occasionally to prevent clumping of fruit.

Use a fine-mesh strainer to strain out solids. Discard. Transfer liqueur to clean container, cover, and let stand for 2 to 3 weeks. Rack or filter liqueur into final container such as wine bottle, fruit jar, or decanter. YIELD: APPROX. 1½ QUARTS

Cherry Liqueurs

The character, color, and flavor of a cherry liqueur depend on the type of cherries used. Royal Ann cherries are mellow and golden; sour cherries — also called pie cherries — are tart and bright red; burgundy cherries — also called Bing cherries — are rich, sweet, and deep red. For a liqueur with a little zing, use pie cherries. For one with a deep golden color, Royal Gold Liqueur will please both your eye and your palate.

Royal Gold Liqueur

1½ cups sugar
1 cup water
1½ pounds fresh golden cherries with pits, stemmed and washed
2 cups sweet white wine
1½ cups brandy
1 teaspoon orange zest
2 tablespoons fresh-squeezed lemon juice

Make a simple syrup by bringing sugar and water to a boil over medium-high heat, stirring constantly to prevent scorching. When clear, remove from heat and let stand until just warm. Cut cherries in half but don't remove pits. Put cherries and pits in clean 2-quart container with tight-fitting lid. Pour syrup over cherries and add wine, brandy, orange zest, and lemon juice. Cover and let stand in a cool, dark place for 1 month, shaking 2 to 3 times a week.

Use a fine-mesh strainer to strain out solids. Discard. Transfer liqueur to clean container, cover, and let stand for 1 week. Rack or filter into final container such as wine bottle, fruit jar, or decanter. YIELD: APPROX. 1½ QUARTS

Cherry Liqueur QUICK & EASY

1½ cups sugar
1 cup water
1½ teaspoons concentrated cherry flavoring extract
1½ cups 100-proof vodka

Make a simple syrup by bringing sugar and water to a boil over medium-high heat, stirring constantly to prevent scorching. When clear, remove from heat and let stand until just warm. Pour into clean 1-quart jar with tight-fitting lid. Add flavoring and vodka, cover, and shake well. This cordial may be served immediately, but it's better if allowed to age for 1 month. YIELD: APPROX. 1 FIFTH

Grapefruit Liqueur

If your vision of a grapefruit liqueur is more salty dog than sweet and smooth, you're in for a surprise when you make this one. It's mellower than you'd expect.

1½	cups sugar
1	cup fumé blanc or other dry white wine
¼	cup pink grapefruit zest
1	teaspoon orange zest
½	cup fresh-squeezed grapefruit juice
1¼	cups 100-proof vodka
1	drop red food coloring

Make a simple syrup by bringing sugar and water to a boil over medium-high heat, stirring constantly to prevent scorching. When clear, remove from heat and let stand until just warm. Pour into clean 1-quart fruit jar with tight-fitting lid. Add grapefruit zest, orange zest, grapefruit juice, vodka, and food coloring. Cover and let stand in a cool, dark place for 1 month.

Rack or filter liqueur into final container such as wine bottle, fruit jar, or decanter. YIELD: APPROX. 1 QUART

Cupid and Cordials
Pretty pink grapefruit liqueur in a cut-glass cruet, a red-wrapped round of Gouda cheese, some crispy crackers tied up in red cellophane and nestled in a little white basket lined with red checked gingham — that says happy Valentine's Day. Tuck in two tiny liqueur glasses, and you may be invited to share.

Versatile Citrus

We like to keep citrus cordials on hand because they're so versatile. They are light and lively, and add sparkle to almost any beverage. They liven up tea, mix well with other fruit liqueurs, and, in small quantities, can be used as a flavoring component in a variety of recipes from fish to frostings. They are also wonderful straight from the bottle.

Lemon Liqueur

This lively liqueur may be a good choice for your first attempt at making cordials.

> 1 cup water
> 2 cups sugar
> 3 tablespoons lemon zest
> ¼ cup fresh-squeezed lemon juice
> 1½ cups 100-proof vodka
> 5–10 drops yellow food coloring

Make a simple syrup by bringing sugar and water to a boil over medium-high heat, stirring constantly to prevent scorching. When clear, remove from heat and let stand until just warm. Pour into clean 2-quart jar with tight-fitting lid. Add lemon zest, lemon juice, vodka, and food coloring. Cover and let stand in a cool, dark place for 1 month.

Rack or filter liqueur into final container such as wine bottle, fruit jar, or decanter. YIELD: APPROX. 1 QUART

Lemon Liqueur

> 1½ cups sugar
> 1 cup water
> ¾ teaspoon lemon flavoring oil
> 1½ cups 100-proof vodka

Make a simple syrup by bringing sugar and water to a boil over medium-high heat, stirring constantly to prevent scorching. When clear, remove from heat and let stand until just warm. Pour into clean 1-quart jar with tight-fitting lid. Add flavoring and vodka, cover, and shake well. This cordial may be served immediately, but it's better if allowed to age for 1 month. YIELD: APPROX. 1 FIFTH

Lime Liqueur

Lime liqueur is a little more tart and acidic than lemon liqueur, but it's wonderful mixed with club soda, sipped from a glass filled with crushed ice, or added to iced tea.

1¼	cups sugar
1	cup water
3	tablespoons lime zest
¼	cup fresh-squeezed lime juice
1½	cups 100-proof vodka
6	drops green food coloring

Make a simple syrup by bringing sugar and water to a boil over medium-high heat, stirring constantly to prevent scorching. When clear, remove from heat and let stand until just warm. Pour into clean 1-quart jar with tight-fitting lid. Add lime zest, lime juice, vodka, and food coloring. Cover and let stand in a cool, dark place for 1 month.

Rack or filter liqueur into final container such as wine bottle, fruit jar, or decanter. YIELD: APPROX. 1 QUART

Lime Liqueur

1½	cups sugar
1	cup water
¾	teaspoon lime flavoring oil
1½	cups 100-proof vodka

Make a simple syrup by bringing sugar and water to a boil over medium-high heat, stirring constantly to prevent scorching. When clear, remove from heat and let stand until just warm. Pour into clean 1-quart jar with tight-fitting lid. Add flavoring and vodka, cover, and shake well. This cordial may be served immediately, but it's better if allowed to age for 1 month. YIELD: APPROX. 1 FIFTH

Orange Liqueur

Orange Liqueur is warmer, softer, and mellower than its citrus cousins. We think this cordial is captivating over crushed ice, congenial in butter icing, and pretty enough to grace any table. We like to serve it with almond cookies, either alone or mixed with coffee for a creative cappuccino.

1½ cups sugar
1 cup water
¼ cup orange zest
2 tablespoons fresh-squeezed lemon juice
1½ cups 80-proof vodka
3 drops yellow food coloring
2 drops red food coloring

Make a simple syrup by bringing sugar and water to a boil over medium-high heat, stirring constantly to prevent scorching. When clear, remove from heat and let stand until just warm. Pour into clean 1-quart jar with tight-fitting lid. Add orange zest, lemon juice, vodka, and food coloring. Cover and let stand in a cool, dark place for 1 month.

Rack or filter liqueur into final container such as wine bottle, fruit jar, or decanter. YIELD: APPROX. 1 QUART

Orange Liqueur

1½ cups sugar
1 cup water
¾ teaspoon orange flavoring oil
1½ cups 100-proof vodka

Make a simple syrup by bringing sugar and water to a boil over medium-high heat, stirring constantly to prevent scorching. When clear, remove from heat and let stand until just warm. Pour into clean 1-quart jar with tight-fitting lid. Add flavoring and vodka, cover, and shake well. This cordial may be served immediately, but it's better if allowed to age for 1 month. YIELD: APPROX. 1 FIFTH

Green Melon Liqueur

    2¼ cups melon syrup
    1¼ cups 100-proof vodka
     ¼ cup water
     1 tablespoon fresh-squeezed lemon juice

Place syrup, vodka, water, and lemon juice in clean 1-quart container. Cover tightly and shake well. Let stand in a cool, dark place for at least 1 month before serving. YIELD: APPROX. 1 FIFTH

Melon Liqueurs

Melons, we thought, should be among the easiest fruits to turn into liqueurs. They are simple to cut up, you get a lot of juice for your effort, and they taste good. We were wrong. Our high expectations for melon-flavored cordials were never realized. It's hard to tell what flavors are inside those deceptive rinds, so rather than thump, sniff, weigh, and hope to get lucky, we decided to try commercial flavorings. The results were more predictable, and the process was certainly easier.

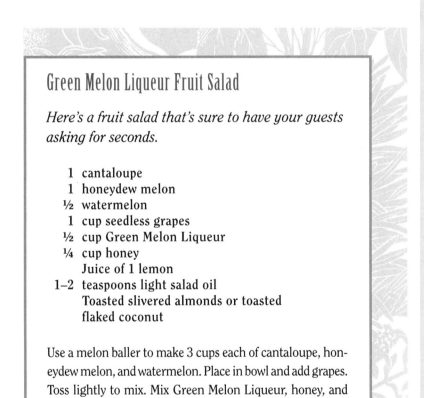

Green Melon Liqueur Fruit Salad

Here's a fruit salad that's sure to have your guests asking for seconds.

      1 cantaloupe
      1 honeydew melon
     ½ watermelon
      1 cup seedless grapes
     ½ cup Green Melon Liqueur
     ¼ cup honey
        Juice of 1 lemon
    1–2 teaspoons light salad oil
        Toasted slivered almonds or toasted
        flaked coconut

Use a melon baller to make 3 cups each of cantaloupe, honeydew melon, and watermelon. Place in bowl and add grapes. Toss lightly to mix. Mix Green Melon Liqueur, honey, and lemon juice. Add salad oil (to help dressing cling to the fruit). Scoop salad into wide-mouthed wineglasses and pour dressing over salad. Top with toasted slivered almonds or toasted flaked coconut. SERVES 10–15.

Patience Is a Virtue

It's tempting to serve cordials made with flavoring agents immediately, since they *look* ready. Because you have not used whole fruits, they do not have to sit in order to clear. Be patieint: As with other cordials, they'll taste better once time has worked its flavor-mellowing magic.

Watermelon Liqueur

Watermelon says summer better than any other fruit we know, but unless you're a fan of watermelon pickles, attempts at preserving watermelon are usually less than satisfactory. Making watermelon liqueur seemed a good solution to the problem of preserving that sweet summer flavor. Our first attempts were, however, just as unsatisfactory as trying to can or freeze the melon. Something got lost in the translation. Then we tried the watermelon flavoring extract that candy makers sometimes use. Bingo! A watermelon cordial that we can serve to guests without damaging our cordial reputation.

   1½ teaspoons watermelon flavoring extract
    1 cup light corn syrup
    1 cup water
   1½ cups 100-proof vodka
    1 tablespoon fruit protector

Place flavoring, corn syrup, water, vodka, and fruit protector in clean 1-quart jar. Cover tightly and shake well. Let stand in a cool, dark place for at least 1 month before serving.

Yield: Approx. 1 fifth

Peach Liqueur

You may decide to keep this liqueur around just for the aroma! It smells like a lazy Georgia afternoon when the peaches are ripe and a soft breeze drifts across the front porch.

- 1 cup sugar
- 1 cup water
- 2 pounds fresh ripe peaches, stemmed and washed
- 1 teaspoon lemon zest
- 1 teaspoon orange zest
- 1½ cups 100-proof vodka
- 1 cup brandy
- 4 drops yellow food coloring

Make a simple syrup by bringing sugar and water to a boil over medium-high heat, stirring constantly to prevent scorching. When clear, remove from heat and let stand until just warm. Cut peaches in half, remove pits, and slice thin. Place peaches, pits, and citrus zests in clean 2-quart jar. Pour syrup over peaches and add vodka, brandy, and food coloring. Cover tightly and let stand in a cool, dark place for 2 weeks.

Use a fine-mesh strainer to strain out solids. Discard. Transfer liqueur to clean container, cover, and let stand for 2 to 3 weeks more. Rack or filter into final container such as wine bottle, fruit jar, or decanter. YIELD: APPROX. 1 QUART

A Unique Flavor
The peach pits give the liqueur a trace of almond flavor.

Peach Liqueur QUICK & EASY

- 1½ cups sugar
- 1 cup water
- 1½ teaspoons concentrated peach flavoring extract
- 1½ cups 100-proof vodka

Make a simple syrup by bringing sugar and water to a boil over medium-high heat, stirring constantly to prevent scorching. When clear, remove from heat and let stand until just warm. Pour into clean 1-quart jar. Add flavoring and vodka, cover tightly, and shake well. Cordial may be served immediately, but it's better if aged for 1 month. YIELD: APPROX. 1 FIFTH

Pear Liqueur

If you like the flavor of plump, ripe pears but dislike their grainy texture, you'll really appreciate the taste of Pear Liqueur — a mellow cordial with all the grace and none of the grit of fresh pears.

    3 cups sugar
    2 cups water
    2 pounds fresh ripe pears, stemmed and washed
    1 teaspoon lemon zest
2½ cups 100-proof vodka
    1 tablespoon fruit protector

Make a simple syrup by bringing sugar and water to a boil over medium-high heat, stirring constantly to prevent scorching. When clear, remove from heat and let stand until just warm. Quarter and core pears, then slice thin. Place pears and lemon zest in clean 2-quart jar with a tight-fitting lid. Pour syrup over pears and add vodka and fruit protector. Cover and let stand in a cool, dark place for 2 weeks.

    Use a fine-mesh strainer to strain out solids. Discard. Transfer liqueur to clean container, cover, and let stand for 2 to 3 weeks more. Rack or filter into final container such as wine bottle, fruit jar, or decanter. YIELD: APPROX. 1½ QUARTS

Prunelle

1 cup sugar
½ cup water
8 large, fresh purple plums, stemmed and washed
3 cups dry white wine
1 cinnamon stick
1 teaspoon pure vanilla extract
1 cup 100-proof vodka

Make a simple syrup by bringing sugar and water to a boil over medium-high heat, stirring constantly to prevent scorching. When clear, remove from heat and let stand until just warm. Pour into clean 2-quart jar with tight-fitting lid. Cut plums in half and remove pits. Add plums, wine, cinnamon, vanilla, and vodka to syrup. Cover and let stand in a cool, dark place for 1 month.

Rack or filter into final container such as wine bottle, fruit jar, or decanter. YIELD: APPROX. 2 QUARTS

Plum Liqueurs

The French call liqueurs made from plums *prunelles*. We've included one French and one Oriental variety here. The French version has a hint of spice; the Oriental is warm, with a taste of honey. Regardless of which one you make, you'll love the rich flavor and beautiful color.

Plum Marinade

For a treat, add the plum residue to a marinade made with teriyaki sauce and a little light vegetable oil. Marinate chicken breasts for several hours. Then pop them into a heavy skillet spritzed with vegetable cooking spray. It may be the lightest and most delicious chicken dish you've ever tasted.

Oriental Plum Liqueur

This liqueur glows with the taste of honey and plums.

> 1 cup water
> 1 cup honey
> 10 fresh yellow plums, stemmed and washed
> 2 cups plum wine
> 1 cup brandy
> 1 cup 100-proof vodka
> ½ teaspoon lemon zest
> 1 tablespoon fresh-squeezed lemon juice

Bring water and honey to a boil over medium-high heat. Boil for 2 to 3 minutes, skimming off any foam that rises to the surface. Remove from heat and let stand until just warm. Pour into clean 2-quart container with tight-fitting lid. Cut plums in half and remove pits. Add pits to jar. Mash plums in a bowl with potato masher. Add mashed plums, wine, brandy, vodka, lemon zest, and lemon juice to syrup. Cover and let stand in a cool, dark place for 1 month.

Use a coarse sieve or colander to strain out solids. Discard. Strain again using a fine-mesh strainer. Transfer to clean container, cover, and let stand for 1 week. Rack or filter into final container such as wine bottle, fruit jar, or decanter.
Yield: Approx. 1½ quarts

Variation: For an interesting variation, try Oriental Spiced Plum Liqueur. Just add the following ingredients to the honey-water mixture.

> 1 teaspoon pure vanilla extract
> ½ teaspoon ground allspice
> ½ teaspoon ground cloves
> ½ teaspoon ground nutmeg
> 2 cinnamon sticks

Rhubarb Liqueur

Rhubarb isn't everyone's cup of tea — or glass of cordial. But something wonderful happens to it when you turn it into this easy-to-make liqueur.

1½	cups water
4	cups fresh rhubarb, cut into 1-inch pieces
3	cups sugar
1	teaspoon orange zest
2	cups 100-proof vodka
2	cups white zinfandel or other rosé wine

Bring water, rhubarb, sugar, and orange zest to a boil over medium-high heat, stirring constantly to prevent scorching. When sugar is dissolved, remove from heat and let stand until just warm. Pour into clean 2-quart jar with tight-fitting lid. Add vodka and wine. Cover and let stand in a cool, dark place for 2 weeks.

Use a fine-mesh strainer to strain out solids. Discard. Transfer liqueur to clean container, cover, and let stand for 2 weeks more. Rack or filter into final container. YIELD: APPROX. 2 QUARTS

Variation, for fans of strawberry-rhubarb pie: Try adding 1 cup crushed strawberries to the cooked rhubarb.

Broiled Grapefruit with Rhubarb Liqueur

Try this as an appetizer for Sunday brunch. Don't worry about the alcohol; it will evaporate in the oven. Halve and section a chilled grapefruit and remove visible seeds. Drain excess juice, then pour 1 tablespoon Rhubarb Liqueur over each half. Sprinkle 1 teaspoon light brown sugar on each half and broil until lightly brown. Sugar should melt but not burn. Top each half with ½ maraschino cherry and serve immediately. Serves 2.

Tropical Liqueurs

Tropical liqueurs are as warm and wonderful as their name suggests. The recipes in this section are made with vodka, which adds little flavor to the finished cordials. Many other tropical liqueurs are made with rum or brandy, and the bases contribute their own flavors. We've included these tropical delights in chapter 8.

Banana Liqueur

Banana Liqueur smells wonderful when you are making it, but the consistency reminds us of pureed baby food. Don't let that put you off. This just may become one of your favorite cordials.

- 1½ cups sugar
- ¾ cup water
- 1 teaspoon pure vanilla extract
- 2 ripe bananas, peeled and mashed
- 3 cups vodka

Make a simple syrup by bringing sugar and water to a boil over medium-high heat, stirring constantly to prevent scorching. When clear, remove from heat and add vanilla. Let stand until just warm. Place mashed banana in clean 1-quart, wide-mouthed jar. Add syrup and vodka. Cover and let stand in a cool, dark place for 3 to 4 days, stirring or shaking once or twice a day to prevent clumping of fruit.

Use a fine-mesh strainer to strain out solids. Discard. The liqueur will still be cloudy. Cover and let stand undisturbed until it clears. Rack into a clean container. Cover and age for 1 month. If more sediment settles to the bottom, rack again before serving. YIELD: APPROX. 1 QUART

Banana Liqueur QUICK & EASY

- 1½ cups sugar
- 1 cup water
- 1½ teaspoons concentrated banana flavoring extract
- 1½ cups 100-proof vodka

Make a simple syrup by bringing sugar and water to a boil over medium-high heat, stirring constantly to prevent scorching. When clear, remove from heat and let stand until just warm. Pour into clean 1-quart jar. Add flavoring and vodka, cover tightly, and shake well. This cordial may be served immediately, but it's better if aged for 1 month. YIELD: APPROX. 1 FIFTH

Banana Parfait

If you're a fan of banana-nut ice cream, try a banana liqueur parfait. In a parfait glass, swirl a little of the cordial with vanilla ice cream and layer with chopped walnuts or macadamia nuts.

Refreshing Kiwi

Kiwi liqueur is a bit like that made from strawberries in that it is refreshing and mildly reminiscent of spring — light, lively, and luscious.

Kiwi Liqueur

Kiwifruits always remind us of a kid who needs a haircut. They may be charming on the inside, but it's hard to take them seriously with all that hair. Who would have thought that they could turn into such a sophisticated cordial!

6	kiwifruits, peeled
2	cups sugar
½	teaspoon orange zest
½	teaspoon lemon zest
2	tablespoons fresh-squeezed lemon juice
1	cup water
1½	cups 100-proof vodka
1	drop green food coloring

Coarsely chop kiwifruit and place in bowl with sugar. Let stand for about 1 hour. Add orange zest, lemon zest, and lemon juice. Transfer to a clean 2-quart container and add water, vodka, and food coloring. Cover and let stand in a cool, dark place for 2 to 3 weeks, shaking occasionally.

Use a fine-mesh strainer to strain out solids. Discard. Transfer liqueur to clean container, cover, and let stand for 1 week. Rack into final container. Age for at least 1 month before serving.
YIELD: APPROX. 1 QUART

Pineapple Liqueur

The best way to ensure good pineapple liqueur is to choose your pineapple carefully. It should be yellow to golden orange in color, and exude the enticing aroma of ripe pineapple.

2   cups sugar
1   cup water
2   cups chopped fresh pineapple
1   teaspoon lemon zest
2   tablespoons fresh-squeezed lemon juice
2   cups 100-proof vodka
4   drops yellow food coloring

Make a simple syrup by bringing sugar and water to a boil over medium-high heat, stirring constantly to prevent scorching. When clear, remove from heat and add pineapple. Cool until just warm. Transfer to clean 1-quart, wide-mouthed jar and add lemon zest, lemon juice, vodka, and food coloring. Cover and let stand in a cool, dark place for 3 to 4 days, stirring or shaking once or twice a day to prevent clumping of fruit.

Use a fine-mesh strainer to strain out solids. Discard or reserve for future use. The liqueur will still be cloudy. Cover and let stand undisturbed until it clears. Rack into clean container and let stand for 1 month. If more sediment settles, rack into final container before serving. YIELD: APPROX. 1 QUART

Cooking with Pineapple

This liqueur is great for cooking, especially with chicken or pork. Use the pineapple chunks that you strain out to cover chicken pieces. Bake for a wonderfully flavorful dish.

Pineapple Liqueur QUICK & EASY

1½ cups sugar
1   cup water
1½ teaspoons pineapple flavoring extract
1½ cups 100-proof vodka

Make a simple syrup by bringing sugar and water to a boil over medium-high heat, stirring constantly to prevent scorching. When clear, remove from heat and let stand until just warm. Pour into clean 1-quart jar. Add flavoring and vodka, cover tightly, and shake well. Cordial may be served immediately, but it's better if aged for 1 month. YIELD: APPROX. 1 FIFTH

Pomegranate Liqueur

Pomegranates have a wonderful flavor and beautiful color, but eating the fresh fruit is a time-consuming endeavor. Pomegranate liqueur gives you the same essence without the trouble.

  3–4 fresh pomegranates
    2 cups sugar
    1 teaspoon orange zest
    1 tablespoon fresh-squeezed lemon juice
    2 cups 100-proof vodka
    1 cup white zinfandel

Peel pomegranates and scrape the flesh-covered seeds into bowl, removing the bits of membrane that separate the seed clusters. Add sugar and crush fruit with wooden spoon. Let stand for about 30 minutes. Add orange zest and lemon juice and let stand for 30 minutes more. Use a fine-mesh strainer to strain out solids. Discard. If necessary, add a little water to the mixture to make 1 cup. Transfer juice to clean 1-quart, wide-mouthed jar with tight-fitting lid. Add vodka and wine. Cover and let stand in a cool, dark place for 1 month.

    Rack or filter into final container such as wine bottle, fruit jar, or decanter. YIELD: APPROX. 1 QUART

Pomegranate Liqueur QUICK & EASY

  1½ cups grenadine
   ½ cup water
  1½ cups 80-proof vodka
    1 teaspoon orange zest
    1 tablespoon fresh-squeezed lemon juice

Combine grenadine, water, vodka, orange zest, and lemon juice in 1-quart jar with tight-fitting lid. Cover and shake well. This cordial may be served immediately, but it's bettter if allowed to age for 1 month. YIELD: APPROX. 1 FIFTH

CHAPTER 3

SOMETHING NUTTY

A fter making a number of fruit-flavored liqueurs, we thought that making other liqueurs would be fairly straightforward. We tried a number of nutty combinations; some were wonderful, others were not. Here are a few tips for those of you who would like to experiment on your own in addition to trying some of our successes.

First, unlike most fruits, it is hard to tell whether nuts are fresh. Nuts are high in oil, and old oil tastes rancid. If you buy shelled nuts in bulk, make sure your source sells a lot of them. Sort the nuts you are going to use in your liqueurs carefully. With a little practice, you'll be able to tell when there's a bad nut in the bunch. Discard any that look shriveled. If you find any that are questionable, break off a piece and taste it.

If you buy nuts in the shell and crack them yourself, be sure not to include any of the membrane that divides the kernels. These membranes are high in tannin. In wine, tannin adds a hint of dryness, and it improves a wine's keeping quality. Some liqueurs benefit from a hint of tannin, but nut cordials aren't among them. Nut cordials should be smooth, sweet, and mellow.

Nuts come in a wide variety of styles — dry roasted, toasted, salted, spiced, smoked, sugarcoated, and simply shelled. Although one or two recipes for nut cordials have a little salt, the vast majority use plain shelled nuts. The flavor of a nut cordial improves if the nuts are toasted in a moderate (350°F) oven, or in a sauté pan over low heat for a few minutes, but beware of scorching. Finally, oil often forms on top of nut liqueur. You can shake the liqueur to disperse it before serving, or you can put the liqueur into the freezer to partially solidify the oil, and skim it off with a small ladle.

Almond Liqueurs

These are among the most popular and most familiar nut-flavored liqueurs. Smooth, mellow, and satisfying, almond liqueurs are popular even with folks who don't normally indulge in cordials.

Almond Liqueur

1 pound shelled almonds
1 cup 100-proof vodka
1 cup brandy
1 cup sugar
½ cup water
2 teaspoons pure vanilla extract
1 teaspoon glycerin (optional)
Caramel coloring

Coarsely chop almonds in food processor. Transfer to clean 1-quart container and add vodka and brandy. Cover and let stand in a cool, dark place for 1 month, shaking or stirring every couple of days. Use coarse sieve or colander to strain out solids. Strain again using a fine mesh strainer. Transfer liqueur to clean jar, cover, and let stand for 2 days more. Rack into clean jar. Make a simple syrup by bringing sugar and water to a boil over medium-high heat, stirring constantly to prevent scorching. When clear, remove from heat and let stand until just warm. Add syrup, vanilla, and glycerin (if using) to racked liqueur. Add caramel coloring drop by drop, stirring after each addition, until desired color is achieved. This cordial may be served immediately, but it's better if aged for 1 to 2 months in a covered jar. YIELD: APPROX. 1 QUART

Almond Roca Liqueur QUICK & EASY

1 cup light brown sugar, loosely packed
½ cup water
1 cup 100-proof vodka
½ cup brandy
¾ cups Torani Almond Roca syrup

Make a simple syrup by bringing sugar and water to a boil over medium-high heat, stirring constantly to prevent scorching. When clear, remove from heat and let stand until just warm. Pour into clean 1-quart container. Add vodka, brandy, and Almond Roca syrup. This cordial is best if allowed to age for 1 to 2 months in a covered container. YIELD: APPROX. 1 FIFTH

Amaretto

This is a more elegant and complex liqueur than Almond Liqueur. The fruit flavors complement the luscious almond flavor and add a hint of golden color to the final product.

½ pound shelled almonds
3 dried apricots
1 teaspoon orange zest
1 teaspoon lemon zest
1 teaspoon fresh-squeezed lemon juice
1½ cups 80-proof vodka
1½ cups brandy
1 cup sugar
½ cup water
2 teaspoons almond extract
1 teaspoon pure vanilla extract
1 teaspoon glycerin (optional)
Caramel coloring

Nut Liqueurs

Nut liqueurs keep well and are so versatile that you'll want to keep several on hand for sipping, sundaes, and parfaits; slipping into dessert recipes; using in sophisticated marinades for chicken and fish; seasoning tea and coffee; and giving to family and friends.

Coarsely chop almonds and apricots in food processor. Place in clean 1-quart container and add orange zest, lemon zest, lemon juice, vodka, and brandy. Cover and let stand in a cool, dark place for 6 weeks.

Use a coarse sieve or colander to strain out solids. Discard. Strain again using a fine-mesh strainer. Transfer liqueur to clean container, cover, and let stand for 2 days. Rack or filter into clean container.

Make a simple syrup by bringing sugar and water to a boil over medium-high heat, stirring constantly to prevent scorching. When clear, remove from heat and let stand until just warm. Add syrup, almond extract, vanilla, and glycerin (if using) to racked liqueur. Add caramel coloring a drop at a time, stirring after each addition, until desired color is achieved. This cordial may be served immediately, but it's better if allowed to age for 1 to 2 months in a covered container. YIELD: APPROX. 1 QUART

Hazelnut Liqueur

Of all the liqueurs we made while preparing this book, this one was the most popular with everyone who tasted it. We simply couldn't keep it on hand.

½ pound hazelnuts
1 cup vodka
½ cup brandy
½ cup white sugar
½ cup light brown sugar
1¼ cups water
1 teaspoon pure vanilla extract
1 teaspoon glycerin (optional)
Caramel coloring

Using Your Hazelnut Liqueur

This recipe is great for sipping, super in frothed warm milk, sinfully delicious mixed with half-and-half, and warm and wonderful added to freshly brewed coffee. It makes a great parfait, too.

Coarsely chop hazelnuts in food processor. Transfer to clean 1-quart container and add vodka and brandy. Cover and store in a cool, dark place for 6 weeks.

Use a coarse sieve or colander to strain out solids. Discard. Strain again with a fine-mesh strainer. Transfer liqueur to clean container, cover, and let stand for 2 days. Rack or filter into clean container.

Make a simple syrup by bringing white sugar, brown sugar, and water to a boil over medium-high heat, stirring constantly to prevent scorching. Remove from heat and let stand until just warm. Add syrup, vanilla, and glycerin (if using) to racked liqueur. Add caramel coloring a drop at a time, stirring after each addition, until desired color is achieved. This cordial may be served immediately, but it's better if allowed to age for 1 to 2 months in a covered container. YIELD: APPROX. 1 FIFTH

Hazelnut Liqueur QUICK & EASY

½ cup sugar
¾ cup water
1 cup 100-proof vodka
½ cup brandy
¾ cup hazelnut syrup
½ teaspoon pure vanilla extract

Make a simple syrup by bringing sugar and water to a boil over medium-high heat, stirring constantly to prevent scorching. When clear, remove from heat and let stand until just warm. Pour into clean 1-quart container and add vodka, brandy, hazelnut syrup, and vanilla. This cordial may be served immediately, but it's better if allowed to age for 1 to 2 months in a covered container. YIELD: APPROX. 1 FIFTH

Tropical Taste

If your budget won't allow for a trip to Hawaii, how about a taste of Hawaii instead? Make a batch of Macadamia Nut Liqueur, tune up the ukulele, and tuck your gift into a decorative basket along with a fresh pineapple and a CD of Hawaiian music. A few sips, a little island music — and you're ready for the luau.

Macadamia Nut Liqueur QUICK & EASY

½ cup sugar
½ cup water
1 cup 100-proof vodka
½ cup brandy
¾ cup macadamia nut syrup
½ teaspoon pure vanilla extract

Make a simple syrup by bringing sugar and water to a boil over medium-high heat, stirring constantly to prevent scorching. When clear, remove from heat and let stand until just warm. Pour into clean 1-quart container and add vodka, brandy, macadamia nut syrup, and vanilla. This cordial may be served immediately, but it's better if allowed to age for 1 to 2 months in a covered container. YIELD: APPROX. 1 FIFTH

Pecan Liqueurs

There are dozens of ways to enjoy pecan liqueurs in addition to sipping them. Here is one of our favorites, Pecan Nut Spread. Soften an 8-ounce package of cream cheese. Blend 2 tablespoons of pecan liqueur into the cream cheese with a fork and stir in 2 tablespoons chopped pecans. Use on bagels, pumpkin bread, banana bread, zucchini bread, Danish pastries, celery sticks, with butter icings — you get the idea.

Pecan Liqueur *QUICK & EASY*

Forget your diet and add this wonderful liqueur to hot chocolate on a cold winter night. Or sip it over ice on a hot summer afternoon. No matter how you serve it, this cordial will warm your innards and raise your spirits.

- 1 cup vodka
- 1 cup brandy
- 1½ teaspoons concentrated pecan flavoring extract
- ½ teaspoon orange zest
- ⅓ cup white sugar
- ⅔ cup light brown sugar
- ¼ teaspoon salt
- ½ cup water

Combine vodka, brandy, flavoring, and orange zest in clean 1-quart jar. Make a simple syrup by bringing white sugar, brown sugar, salt, and water to a boil over medium-high heat, stirring constantly to prevent scorching. Remove from heat and let stand until just warm. Combine with alcohol mixture. Let stand in a cool, dark place for at least 1 month in a covered container.
YIELD: APPROX. 1 FIFTH

Butter Pecan Liqueur *QUICK & EASY*

This delicious cordial has all the warmth we've come to associate with soft southern evenings, when the front-porch swing creaks, the crickets sing, and the setting sun casts a golden spell over the yard.

- 1 cup vodka
- 1 cup brandy
- 3 teaspoons concentrated pecan flavoring extract
- ¾ teaspoon butter flavoring extract
- ½ teaspoon orange zest
- ⅓ cup white sugar
- ⅔ cup light brown sugar
- ¼ teaspoon salt
- ½ cup water

Combine vodka, brandy, pecan flavoring, butter flavoring, and orange zest in clean 1-quart jar. Make a simple syrup by bringing white sugar, brown sugar, salt, and water to a boil over medium-high heat, stirring constantly to prevent scorching. When clear, remove from heat and let stand until just warm. Combine with alcohol mixture. Let age for at least 1 month in a covered container. YIELD: APPROX. 1 FIFTH

Spiced Pecan Liqueur

This liqueur, which combines a mellow pecan flavor with zippy spices, was particularly popular with our tasters. You can use it to make some of the most delicious brandied fruits we've ever tried. It's also downright dangerous in a wide variety of teas.

1	cup vodka
1	cup brandy
1½	teaspoons pecan flavoring extract
½	teaspoon orange zest
⅓	cup white sugar
⅔	cup light brown sugar
½	cup water
1	cinnamon stick
3	whole cloves
½	teaspoon ground allspice

Combine vodka, brandy, flavoring, and orange zest in clean 1-quart jar. Make a simple syrup by bringing the white sugar, brown sugar, and water to a boil over medium-high heat, stirring constantly to prevent scorching. Tie cinnamon, cloves, and allspice in cheesecloth and add to syrup. When clear, remove from heat and let stand until just warm. Add syrup and spices to alcohol mixture. Cover and let stand in a cool, dark place for 1 month.

Remove and discard spice bag. Transfer liqueur to clean, covered container. YIELD: APPROX. 1 FIFTH

Serving Suggestions
Butter Pecan Liqueur is wonderful with a slice of homemade peach pie or as a tasty addition to tea or coffee.

Pistachio Liqueur QUICK & EASY

There are pistachio people and nonpistachio people. We're willing to bet that there will be more of the former once they taste this liqueur.

    2 cups 80-proof vodka
    ¾ teaspoon pistachio flavoring extract
    1 cup sugar
    ½ cup water
    1 teaspoon glycerin (optional)
    4 drops green food coloring

Combine vodka and flavoring in clean 1-quart jar. Make a simple syrup by bringing sugar and water to a boil over medium-high heat, stirring constantly to prevent scorching. When clear, remove from heat and let stand until just warm. Add syrup, glycerin (if using), and green food coloring to alcohol mixture. Cover and let stand in a cool, dark place for at least 1 month.
YIELD: APPROX. 1 FIFTH

Pistachio Parfait

Layers of Pistachio Liqueur, vanilla ice cream, and pistachio ice cream in a tall parfait glass make one of the prettiest — and easiest — desserts you can serve.

Pour 1 tablespoon of Pistachio Liqueur into a parfait glass. Alternate teaspoons of vanilla and pistachio ice cream until glass is half full. Add 1 tablespoon Pistachio Liqueur and continue alternating ice creams. When there is an inch of space left, add 1 tablespoon liqueur, a dollop of whipped cream, and top with toasted, chopped pistachios and a cherry.

Black Walnut Liqueur

Both black walnuts and English walnuts make excellent liqueurs. Black walnut flavor is intense and distinctive, and the nuts are very hard to crack. For advice on cracking and toasting walnuts, see sidebars at the right.

1   cup shelled black walnuts
1   cup 100-proof vodka
½   cup bourbon
1½ cups light corn syrup
½   cup water
1   teaspoon pure vanilla extract

Toast walnuts. Transfer to clean 1-quart jar with tight-fitting lid. Add vodka and bourbon and cover tightly right away so alcohol doesn't evaporate. Let stand in a cool, dark place for 1 month, shaking occasionally.

Use a fine-mesh strainer to strain out walnuts. Discard. Transfer liqueur to clean container. Bring corn syrup and water to a boil over medium-high heat, stirring constantly to prevent scorching. Remove from heat and let stand until just warm. Add syrup and vanilla to liqueur, cover, and age for 1 month.
YIELD: APPROX. 1 QUART

Black Walnut Liqueur   QUICK & EASY

1   cup vodka
1   cup brandy
1½ teaspoons concentrated black walnut flavoring extract
1   cup sugar
½   cup water

Combine vodka, brandy, and favoring in clean 1-quart jar. Make a simple syrup by bringing sugar and water to a boil over medium-high heat, stirring constantly to prevent scorching. When clear, remove from heat and let stand until just warm. Add to alcohol mixture. Cover and let stand in a cool, dark place for at least 1 month. YIELD: APPROX. 1 FIFTH

Toasting Walnuts

To toast the nuts, preheat oven to 350°F. Spread shelled nuts on a cookie sheet and bake until lightly toasted. You can also toast nuts over medium heat in a heavy saucepan or sauté pan on top of the stove, tossing until lightly toasted. We prefer the stove-top method, which makes it easier to toast the nuts evenly.

Cracking Black Walnuts

Wear gloves to remove the tough, green jackets, or you may find yourself with dark brown fingers for days afterward.

The nuts themselves are encased in tough, wrinkly shells. You may need an "industrial-strength" nutcracker. Or spread a heavy plastic sheet over your driveway, scatter the nuts on top, cover with another sheet, and then drive your car over them.

Walnut Cream

No matter which method you use to make Black Walnut Liqueur, combine it with a little half-and-half to make a unique drink.

Toasted English Walnut Liqueur

This is a luscious liqueur! The flavor is less intense than that of black walnut liqueur, for those of you who like your walnut liqueurs laid back and languid.

> 1   cup shelled English walnuts
> 1½   cups brandy
>   1   cup sugar
>   1   cup water
>   ½   cup honey
>   1   teaspoon pure vanilla extract

Toast walnuts. Place in clean 1-quart jar with tight-fitting lid. Add brandy and cover jar immediately to prevent alcohol from evaporating. Store in a cool, dark place for 1 month, shaking occasionally.

Use a fine-mesh strainer to strain out walnuts. Discard. Transfer liqueur to clean container. Bring sugar, water, and honey to a boil over medium-high heat, stirring constantly to prevent scorching. Skim off any foam that rises to the top. Remove from heat and let stand until just warm. Add syrup and vanilla to liqueur and age for 1 month. YIELD: APPROX. 1 QUART

Toasted Walnut Liqueur QUICK & EASY

Rich walnut flavor — and ready in a jiffy.

> 1   cup toasted walnut syrup
> 1   cup vodka
> 1   cup brandy
> ½   cup honey

Combine syrup, vodka, brandy, and honey in clean 1-quart jar. Cover and age for at least 1 month before serving. YIELD: APPROX. 1 FIFTH

Spiced Honey-Walnut Liqueur

Inspired by some Greek pastries we sampled at a Greek festival, this liqueur is a perfect accompaniment to Mediterranean meals and is wonderful with baklava.

1	cup shelled English walnuts
1½	cups brandy
1	cinnamon stick
3	whole cloves
1	cup water
1	cup honey
1	teaspoon pure vanilla extract
1	teaspoon orange zest
1	teaspoon lemon zest

Toast walnuts. Place in clean 1-quart jar with tight-fitting lid. Add brandy and cover jar immediately to prevent alcohol from evaporating. Store in a cool, dark place for 1 month, shaking occasionally.

Use a fine-mesh strainer to strain out walnuts. Discard. Transfer liqueur to clean container. Bring water and honey to a boil over medium-high heat. Boil for 2 to 3 minutes, skimming off any foam that rises to the surface. Remove from heat and add cinnamon and cloves. Let stand until just warm. Add vanilla, orange zest, and lemon zest. Add syrup to liqueur, cover, and let stand for 2 days. Use fine-mesh strainer to strain out solids. Discard. This cordial may be served immediately, but it's better if allowed to age for at least 1 month in a covered container.
YIELD: APPROX. 1 FIFTH

Removing Beeswax
The foam that forms when the honey mixture is boiled will contain any beeswax left in the honey. Skimming that foam removes the beeswax from your liqueur.

CHAPTER 4

HERB AND SPICE CORDIALS

Herb and spice cordials are the oldest and most sophisticated liqueurs. When they were first created by alchemists sometime before the thirteenth century, they were thought to be medicinal, and they surely must have made those who tasted them feel better. With the addition of sweeteners to improve their taste, even those who didn't need these good-tasting elixers were soon drinking the liqueurs. As you experiment with your own favorite flavors, you'll be following in the long tradition of monks and alchemists, who guarded their special recipes with great zeal.

Most of our recipes call for dried herbs because their flavors are more concentrated than those of fresh herbs. If you decide to use your own homegrown herbs, whether fresh or dried, you will need to taste-test your cordials, as the intensity of the herbs' flavors may vary considerably depending on growing conditions. Herbs that grow in poor, dry soils often have more intense flavors than those that are lovingly fertilized and watered.

We find the distinction between herbs and spices somewhat vague. Leaves, stems, flowers and berries, seeds and bark, and resins such as balsamite and myrrh sometimes flavor liqueurs. We've also had good luck with liqueurs made with various teas.

Common Herbal Liqueur Flavorings

Aloe
Angelica root
Arnica
Artemisia
Balsamite
Dill seed
Fennel seed
Gentian
Ginseng root
Hyssop
Juniper berries
Licorice root
Maidenhair
Melissa
Mint
Orrisroot
Pimento (allspice berry)
Rose hips
Rosemary
Saffron
Sage
Tea
Thyme
Verbena

Angelica Liqueur

Angelica root was used extensively in ancient times to protect one from the plague and ward off evil spirits. Angelica's flavor comes from an oil that is present primarily in the root. It is used in the production of vermouth, Chartreuse, and gin.

  1 cup vodka
  ½ cup brandy
  3 tablespoons finely chopped dried angelica root
  1 tablespoon chopped almonds
  4 dried apricots, chopped
  ⅛ teaspoon ground allspice
  ⅛ teaspoon ground cinnamon
  1 teaspoon anise extract
  ⅛ teaspoon powdered coriander seed
  1 cup sugar
1½ cups water
  1 drop yellow food coloring
  1 drop green food coloring

Combine vodka, brandy, angelica, almonds, apricots, allspice, cinnamon, anise extract, and coriander in 1-quart jar with tight-fitting lid. Cover and let stand in a cool, dark place for 2 weeks, shaking frequently to prevent clumping.

    Use a fine-mesh strainer to strain out solids. Discard. Make a simple syrup by bringing sugar and water to a boil over medium-high heat, stirring frequently to prevent scorching. When clear, remove from heat and let stand until just warm. Add food coloring; then add syrup to vodka mixture. Cover and age for at least 1 month. Rack or filter liqueur into final container.

YIELD: APPROX. 1 FIFTH

Anisette

Anisette is one of the sweetest liqueurs available, with a sugar content generally around 40 percent. It usually contains only 25 to 30 percent alcohol. Marie Brizard, the largest-selling anisette in France, has a relatively subtle aroma, and its flavor is soft and delicate. Italian and Dutch products are usually heavier, stronger, and sweeter.

>   2 cups 80-proof vodka
>   1 tablespoon anise extract
> 1¾ cups light corn syrup
>   1 teaspoon glycerin (optional)

Pour vodka into bottle in which anisette will be stored. Add anise extract and shake vigorously. Add corn syrup and glycerin (if using) and shake well. Cover and let stand in a cool, dark place for 1 month before serving. YIELD: APPROX. 1 FIFTH

The Anisette Family

Aniseed has a sweet, licorice-like flavor that is warm, relaxing, and tasty. It comes in two well-known varieties: The Chinese variety *(illicium verum)* is from a small evergreen tree found in southwestern China. The Mediterranean variety *(Pimpinella anisum)* grows in the southern Mediterranean region. Anisette is often used as an aperitif.

Serving Anisette

We think anisette is best served super cold. It will remain liquid but ice-cold in your freezer. For a special-occasion centerpiece, place a bottle of anisette in a plastic milk jug with the top cut away, fill the jug with water, and slip it into the freezer. When the water freezes, cut the plastic away and place ice and anisette in a crystal bowl.

Gulliano (Our Version of Galliano)

A sophisticated cousin of anisette, Galliano has a more complex character. This recipe is a fairly accurate re-creation of the original. Since Rich developed it on his own, he took the liberty of giving it his name.

2 teaspoons finely chopped dried angelica root
1 tablespoon anise extract
1 tablespoon pure vanilla extract
1 teaspoon banana extract
1 teaspoon pineapple extract
13 drops tangerine extract*
  Pinch mace
¼ teaspoon cardamom seeds
1 teaspoon dried hyssop
1 teaspoon fruit protector
1¼ cups 100-proof vodka
1½ cups sugar
1¾ cups water

Place angelica, anise extract, vanilla, banana extract, pineapple extract, tangerine extract, mace, cardamom, hyssop, and fruit protector in clean 1-quart jar with tight-fitting lid. Add vodka, cover, and let stand in a cool, dark place for 2 weeks. Shake every couple of days to prevent clumping.

Use a fine-mesh strainer to strain out solids. Discard. Pour liqueur into a clean 1-quart container. Make a simple syrup by bringing the sugar and water to a boil over medium-high heat, stirring constantly to prevent scorching. When clear, remove from heat and let stand until just warm. Add to vodka mixture and stir or shake until blended. Cover and age for 1 month before serving. YIELD: APPROX. 1 QUART

*See next page for making tangerine extract.

Tangerine Extract

If you have trouble finding tangerine extract, you can make it by combining ¼ teaspoon tangerine flavoring oil with 2 tablespoons 100-proof vodka. Of you can substitute ¼ teaspoon orange extract in the recipe.

Perfect with Baklava

One of our friends, who is proud of his Greek heritage, sends us the most delicious baklava for the holidays. This spectacular Greek dessert practically demands a tiny glass of ouzo to accompany it. The strong anise flavor is a perfect foil for the rich, sweet baklava.

Ouzo

Ouzo, the fiery Greek cousin of anisette, has a strong flavor. It is not as sweet as anisette and has a higher alcohol content.

  2¾ cups 100-proof vodka
    4 teaspoons anise extract
    3 tablespoons sugar
    1 cup water
    1 teaspoon glycerin (optional)

Pour vodka into bottle in which ouzo will be stored. Add anise extract and shake vigorously. Add sugar, water, and glycerin (if using) and shake well. Cover and age for 1 month before serving.
YIELD: APPROX. 1 FIFTH

Serving Kümmel

Kümmel, developed in Scandinavia, is — like anisette — a liqueur best served icy cold. We like it with corned beef sandwiches and caraway-flavored sauerkraut. Not many other liqueurs will stand up to such hardy, strong-flavored foods.

Caraway Liqueur (Our Version of Kümmel)

Caraway isn't for everyone, but this liqueur had some ardent supporters in our taste-test group. If you've tried and like Kümmel, you may enjoy this version.

- ¾ cup water
- 1½ cups sugar
- 2 tablespoons caraway seed
- 1 teaspoon fennel seeds
- 1 teaspoon aniseed
- 1 teaspoon coriander seeds
- 1 teaspoon dried angelica root, finely chopped
- 3 whole cloves
- 2½ cups 100-proof vodka

Bring sugar and water to a boil over medium-high heat, stirring constantly to prevent scorching. Add caraway, fennel, aniseed, coriander, angelica, and cloves and boil for 4 minutes. Remove from heat and let stand until just warm. Use a coarse sieve or colander to strain out solids. Discard. Strain again using a fine-mesh strainer. Pour into clean 1-quart container with tight-fitting lid. Add vodka. Cover and let stand in a cool, dark place for 1 month. Rack or filter liqueur into final container.

YIELD: APPROX. 1 QUART

Herb Liqueur Italiano
(Our Version of Strega)

A liqueur produced in the southern Italian town of Benevento, Strega has a strong herbal character similar to the French-style herb liqueurs. Though not an exact replication, this recipe captures the essence of this famous cordial.

    1   cup honey
    1   cup water
    2   teaspoons black cardamom seeds
    3   star anise flowers
    1   tablespoon dried angelica root, finely chopped
    1   cinnamon stick
    ¼   teaspoon ground cloves
    ¼   teaspoon ground mace
    2   teaspoons dried hyssop
    1   tablespoon fresh rosemary leaves
    1   teaspoon lemon zest
    1   teaspoon orange zest
    1   teaspoon pure vanilla extract
    2   cups 100-proof vodka
    6   drops yellow food coloring

Bring honey and water to a boil over medium-high heat. Boil for 2 to 3 minutes, skimming off any foam that rises to the surface. Add cardamom, star anise, angelica, cinnamon, cloves, mace, hyssop, and rosemary. Boil for 4 minutes more; then remove from heat and let stand until just warm. Use a coarse sieve or colander to strain out solids. Discard. Strain again, using a fine-mesh strainer. Pour into a clean 1-quart container with tight-fitting lid. Add lemon zest, orange zest, vanilla, vodka, and food coloring. Cover and let stand in a cool, dark place for 1 month.

Use a fine-mesh strainer to strain out solids. Discard. Transfer liqueur to a clean, covered container and age for 1 week more. Rack or filter liqueur into final container. YIELD: APPROX. 1 QUART

Mint Liqueurs

Mints are herbs with a past. Peppermint tea, described in the Ebers papyrus, the oldest known medical text, is a treatment for upset stomach. The Pharisees paid their tithes to the pharaohs with mint, and ancient Hebrews strewed mint on the floors of their synagogues to freshen the air. Mint also freshens the breath and, some say, lifts up the spirit. Mint liqueurs are among the world's most popular cordials. You can make a number of different varieties:

Apple mint
Bergamot
Corsican mint
Curly mint
Pennyroyal
Peppermint
Pineapple mint
Spearmint

Fresh Mint Liqueur

Use this recipe to create your own version of the classic crème de menthe. Commercial versions are carefully selected blends of different mints from around the world. Experiment with this basic recipe, using the various garden mints, either alone or in combination.

1 cup assorted fresh mint leaves, loosely packed
1 cup 100-proof vodka
½ cup brandy
1 cup sugar
2 cups water
1 teaspoon glycerin (optional)
2 drops green food coloring

To prepare the mint leaves, remove from stems, wash leaves in cold water, then dry gently between paper towels. Coarsely chop mint leaves and place in a clean 1-quart container with a tight-fitting lid. Add vodka and brandy. Cover and let stand in a cool, dark place for 1 week.

Use a fine-mesh strainer to strain out leaves. Discard. Transfer liquid to clean container. Make a simple syrup by bringing sugar and water to a boil over medium-high heat, stirring constantly to prevent scorching. When clear, remove from heat and let stand until just warm. Add to vodka mixture, cover, and age for 1 to 3 months before serving. YIELD: APPROX. 1 FIFTH

Lemon-Mint Liqueur

This liqueur is an exciting addition to a cool pitcher of iced tea garnished with fresh mint sprigs. When your guests ask you what you did to make the tea so wonderful, you can surprise them with a gift of homemade liqueur. You will secure your reputation as a good cook and a thoughtful host with impeccable taste.

- ¾ cup fresh mint leaves, loosely packed
- 1½ cups light rum
- ⅓ cup fresh lemon thyme leaves, loosely packed
- 1 cup sugar
- 2 cups water
- ⅓ cup fresh lemon balm, loosely packed
- ⅓ cup fresh lemongrass
- 2 teaspoons lemon zest

Coarsely chop mint leaves and place in clean 1-quart container with tight-fitting lid. Add rum. Cover and let stand in a cool, dark place for 1 week.

Use a fine-mesh strainer to strain out leaves. Discard. Transfer liquid to a clean container. Coarsely chop lemon thyme leaves and add to rum mixture. Cover tightly and let stand for 1 week.

Use a fine-mesh strainer to strain out leaves. Discard. Transfer liquid to a clean container. Make a simple syrup by bringing sugar and water to a boil over medium-high heat, stirring constantly to prevent scorching. Coarsely chop and add lemon balm and lemongrass and boil for 5 minutes more, stirring frequently. Use a fine-mesh strainer to strain out solids. Discard. Let tea cool for 15 minutes.

Add tea and lemon zest to rum mixture. Cover and age for 1 month. Rack or filter liqueur into final container, cover, and age for 2 months before serving. YIELD: APPROX. 1 FIFTH

Mint Julep Liqueur

When making this liqueur, be sure to use a good-quality Kentucky bourbon; you can definitely taste the difference.

>   1 cup fresh spearmint leaves, firmly packed
> 1½ cups Kentucky bourbon
>   1 cup sugar
>   2 cups water

Coarsely chop mint leaves and place in clean 1-quart container with tight-fitting lid. Add bourbon. Let stand in a cool, dark place for 1 week.

Use a fine-mesh strainer to strain out leaves. Transfer liquid to a clean container. Make a simple syrup by bringing sugar and water to a boil over medium-high heat, stirring constantly to prevent scorching. When clear, remove from heat and let stand until just warm. Add to bourbon mixture. Cover and age for 1 to 3 months before serving. YIELD: APPROX. 1 FIFTH

Derby-Day Julep

Here is perhaps the easiest way to serve mint juleps for a Kentucky Derby party. Pour a bottle of Mint Julep Liqueur into a pitcher of crushed ice and let stand for 15 to 20 minutes to melt the ice. Pour into tall glasses garnished with fresh spearmint sprigs. This will be the smoothest mint julep you'll ever taste.

Colorado Red Herb Liqueur

When we spent a summer in the Colorado mountains several years ago, the favorite filler for the hummingbird feeders was sweetened Red Zinger™ tea. We wouldn't recommend that you feed this liqueur to hummingbirds, but we're willing to bet you'll enjoy this adults-only version of Red Zinger!

    2 cups water
    8 bags Celestial Seasonings Red Zinger Tea™
    1 cinnamon stick, broken into six pieces
    1 tablespoon fresh rosemary leaves
    ⅛ teaspoon ground cloves
    1 cup honey
    2 teaspoons orange zest
    1 cup 100-proof vodka
    ½ cup brandy

Combine water, tea bags, cinnamon, rosemary, and cloves in saucepan. Bring to a boil over medium-high heat and boil for 7 minutes. Use a fine-mesh strainer to strain out solids. Return liquid to saucepan and bring back to a boil. Add honey and boil for 2 to 3 minutes, skimming off any foam that rises to the surface. Pour into a clean 1-quart container with a tight-fitting lid. Add orange zest and let cool for 15 minutes. Add vodka and brandy. Cover and let stand in a cool, dark place for 1 month.

Rack or filter liqueur into final container, cover, and age for 1 month before serving. YIELD: APPROX. 1 QUART

Herbal Tea Liqueurs

In your local supermarket, you can find specialty teas by the dozens with names like Mandarin Orange, Red Zinger, and Black Raspberry. Or you can opt for pure tea flavors such as Jasmine and Oolong. All of them make sweet and subtle cordials. We hope you'll make the recipes below and then create your own favorites.

Rosemary-Tangerine Liqueur

Unwind after a long day with this lovely liqueur.

1 cup sugar
2 cups water
¾ cup fresh rosemary leaves, loosely packed
2 teaspoons tangerine zest
1 cup 80-proof vodka
½ cup brandy

Rosemary Liqueurs

Rosemary is a magical herb. Herbalists say it helps relieve headaches, soothes the digestive system, and helps relieve stress — all this and a tantalizing taste as well.

Bring sugar and water to a boil over medium-high heat, stirring constantly to prevent scorching. Add rosemary leaves and boil for 5 minutes, stirring frequently. Use a fine-mesh strainer to strain out leaves. Discard. Transfer liquid to a clean 1-quart container with a tight-fitting lid. Add tangerine zest and let cool for 15 minutes. Add vodka and brandy. Cover and let stand in a cool, dark place for 1 month.

Rack or filter liqueur into final container, cover, and age for 1 month before serving. YIELD: APPROX. 1 QUART

Rosemary-Tangerine Suggestions

The uses for Rosemary-Tangerine Liqueur are myriad. For starters, try it as a marinade, a flavoring agent in vinaigrette, or an interesting additive to iced tea.

Rosemary-Lavender Liqueur

- 1 cup honey
- 1½ cups water
- 1 cup fresh rosemary leaves, loosely packed
- ½ cup fresh lavender flowers
- ⅛ teaspoon ground cardamom
- 1 teaspoon dried hibiscus flowers
- 2 teaspoons lemon zest
- 2 tablespoons fresh-squeezed lemon juice
- 1 cup 80-proof vodka
- ½ cup brandy

Bring honey and water to a boil over medium-high heat. Boil for 2 to 3 minutes, skimming off foam. Add rosemary, lavender, cardamom, and hibiscus flowers and simmer for 5 minutes more. Strain through fine mesh into clean 1-quart jar, discarding solids. Add lemon zest and juice. Cool. Add vodka and brandy. Cover tightly and let stand in a cool, dark place for 1 month.

Rack or filter liqueur into final container, cover, and age for 1 month before serving. YIELD: APPROX. 1 QUART

Sassafras Liqueur

This liqueur is reminiscent of old-fashioned sassafras tea.

- 1 cup sugar
- 1½ cups water
- ½ cup Pappy's Sassafras Tea Concentrate™
- 1 cup brandy
- ½ cup 100-proof vodka

Make a simple syrup by bringing sugar and water to a boil over medium-high heat, stirring constantly to prevent scorching. When clear, remove from heat and let stand until just warm. Pour syrup, sassafras tea concentrate, brandy, and vodka into clean 1-quart jar. Cover tightly. Let stand in a cool, dark place for 1 month.

Rack or filter liqueur into final container, cover, and age for 1 month before serving. YIELD: APPROX. 1 QUART

Rosemary-Lavender Relaxation

This delicately flavored liqueur is the perfect gift for someone whose taste runs to lace and Victoriana. Fill a lavender-tinted cruet from the Victorian era with Rosemary-Lavender Liqueur. Place it in a container filled with dried lavender and rosemary potpourri. Add purple and lavender ribbon, a bar of lavender soap or bubble bath, and a little drawstring bag containing a tiny liqueur glass. Invite your favorite stressed-out friend to enjoy a soothing soak and a few sips of instant stress relief.

Spice Liqueur Flavorings

Aniseed
Caraway
Cardamom
Chinchona
Cinnamon
Cloves
Coriander seeds
Cumin seeds
Dill seeds
Fennel seeds
Gingerroot
Mace
Nutmeg

Cinnamon Stick Liqueur

1½ cups sugar
1 cup water
2 cinnamon sticks
3 whole cloves
¼ teaspoon ground mace
1 cup 100-proof vodka
½ cup brandy
4 drops red food coloring

Combine sugar, water, cinnamon, cloves, and mace in saucepan and bring to a boil over medium-high heat, stirring frequently to prevent scorching. Boil for 5 minutes, remove from the heat, and let stand until just warm. Pour syrup, vodka, and brandy into clean 1-quart container with tight-fitting lid. Cover and let stand for 1 month.

Rack or filter into final container, cover, and age for 1 month before serving. YIELD: APPROX. 1 QUART

Cinnamon Bam

This liqueur is Rich's rendition of a high-proof cinnamon schnapps. We called it Cinnamon Bam because it has a real kick. It was so popular with our tasters that we suggest you make a double batch.

- 4 bags Celestial Seasonings Bengal Spice Tea™
- 2 cups water
- ½ pound red hots (little red cinnamon-flavored candies)
- 1 dried cayenne pepper or pinch ground cayenne pepper
- 1½ cups pure grain alcohol or 100-proof vodka
- 6 drops red food coloring

Combine water, tea bags, and cayenne in saucepan. Bring to a boil over medium-high heat and boil for 2 minutes. Remove from heat; then remove tea bags and whole cayenne pepper (if using). Add red hots and stir until dissolved. Let stand until just warm. Pour into a clean 1-quart container. Add alcohol or vodka and food coloring. Cover and let age for at least 1 month before serving.

YIELD: APPROX. 1 QUART

A Soothing Spice

Cinnamon is a comfort flavor. It is warm, enticing, and familiar. Cultivated in the West Indies and many Eastern countries, cinnamon comes from the bark of a young tree. Its refreshing, sweet taste cleanses the palate and soothes the stomach, making a cinnamon liqueur the perfect choice for an after-dinner drink. We've added Cinnamon Bam to Mexican hot chocolate, too.

Clove Liqueur

        1   cup sugar
    2½   cups water (approximately), divided
        2   tablespoons whole cloves
        1   tablespoon dried hibiscus flowers
        1   cup 100-proof vodka
        ½   cup brandy
        6   drops caramel coloring

Combine sugar, 1½ cups water, cloves, and hibiscus flowers in a saucepan. Bring to a boil over medium-high heat and boil for 10 minutes, stirring frequently to prevent scorching. If you would like a mildly flavored clove liqueur, use a fine-mesh strainer to strain out solids. If a stronger liqueur is desired, do not strain. Let stand until just warm. Pour into a clean 1-quart container. Add vodka, brandy, and enough water to make 1 quart. Cover and let stand in a cool, dark place for 1 month.

If you're making a mild liqueur, rack or filter it into final container. If you left hibiscus flowers and cloves in the liqueur for a stronger flavor, use a fine-mesh strainer to strain them out. Cover and let stand for 1 week more; then rack or filter liqueur into final container. YIELD: APPROX. 1 QUART

Clove Liqueur QUICK & EASY

        1   cup sugar
        1   cup water
        ¾   teaspoon clove flavoring oil
        1   cup 100-proof vodka
        ½   cup brandy

Make a simple syrup by bringing sugar and water to a boil over medium-high heat, stirring constantly to prevent scorching. When clear, remove from heat and let stand until just warm. Pour into a clean 1-quart container and add flavoring, vodka, and brandy. Cover tightly and shake to mix. Let stand in a cool, dark place for 1 month before serving. YIELD: APPROX. 1 FIFTH

A Brief History of Cloves

Cloves are the dried flower buds of clove trees, which originally grew in the Moluccas. First brought to Europe sometime between the fourth and sixth centuries A.D., cloves have retained their popularity for flavoring foods and treating illnesses. Today, clove oil is still used to reduce the pain associated with toothache.

Liqueur of Love (Coriander)

The primary ingredient in this liqueur is coriander, which was used in love potions during the Middle Ages and the Renaissance. Cultivated for more than 3,000 years, coriander appears in many early medical texts. Now it is used widely as a culinary herb.

- 1 tablespoon coriander seed
- 1 teaspoon cardamom seed
- 1 star anise flower
- 6 whole cloves
- 6 rose hips
- 2 cups water (approximately), divided
- 1 cup honey
- 2 tablespoons dried hibiscus flowers
- 3 teaspoons orange zest
- 1 cup 100-proof vodka
- ½ cup brandy

Coarsely grind coriander, cardamom, star anise, cloves, and rose hips in coffee grinder or food processor. Bring 1 cup water and honey to a boil over medium-high heat. Boil for 2 to 3 minutes, skimming off any foam that rises to the surface. Add spice mixture and boil for 4 minutes more. Remove from heat and let stand for 5 minutes. Place hibiscus flowers in bowl. Use a fine-mesh strainer to strain syrup into bowl. Let stand for 10 minutes, then strain into a clean 1-quart container. Add orange zest, vodka, and brandy. Top off with remaining water. Cover and let stand in a cool, dark place for 1 month. Use a coarse sieve or colander to strain out orange zest. Discard.

Rack or filter liqueur into final container and age for 1 month before serving. YIELD: APPROX. 1 QUART

Ginger Liqueur

In addition to sipping, you'll find dozens of uses for this liqueur — in spice cake, pumpkin pie, frostings, marinades, and Asian cuisine.

1 cup white sugar
½ cup light brown sugar, firmly packed
1¼ cups water
3 tablespoons chopped gingerroot
3 whole cloves
1 teaspoon black cardamom seeds
1 teaspoon orange zest
1 cup 100-proof vodka
½ cup brandy

Ginger Liqueurs

Ginger grows wild in the jungles of Southeast Asia and is now cultivated around the world. It is a mainstay of Eastern cookery and is widely used for baking in Western cultures. In small amounts, it adds a rich, spicy, pungent flavor; in larger amounts, it adds "heat."

Bring white sugar, brown sugar, and water to a boil over medium-high heat. Add gingerroot, cloves, and cardamom and boil for 5 minutes. Remove from heat and let stand until just warm. Use a fine-mesh strainer to strain out solids. Discard. Transfer liquid to a clean 1-quart container. Add orange zest, vodka, and brandy. Cover and let stand in a cool, dark place for 1 month.

Use a fine-mesh strainer to strain out orange zest. Discard. Transfer liqueur to clean container, cover, and let stand for 1 week more. Rack or filter liqueur into final container.
YIELD: APPROX. 1 QUART

Ginger-Honey Liqueur

1 cup honey
1 cup water
3 tablepoons chopped gingerroot
1 teaspoon lemon zest
1½ cups Scotch whiskey

Bring honey and water to a boil over medium-high heat. Boil for 2 to 3 minutes, skimming off any foam that rises to the surface. Add gingerroot and lemon zest. Boil for 4 minutes more. Remove from heat and let stand until just warm. Use a fine-mesh strainer to strain out solids. Discard. Transfer liquid to a clean 1-quart container with tight-fitting lid. Add whiskey. Cover and let stand in a cool, dark place for 1 month.

Rack or filter liqueur into final container and age for 2 weeks before serving. YIELD: APPROX. 1 FIFTH

Ginger-Honey Punch

Here's a quick and easy punch that'll do you proud at your next party.

1 fifth Ginger-Honey Liqueur
1 cup vodka
1 quart orange juice
1 quart ginger ale
1 quart soda
2 sliced oranges
6 pieces star anise

Place a large block of ice in punch bowl. Pour in all ingredients and stir well to mix. Orange slices and star anise will float on top. Garnish with a sprig of fresh mint. SERVES 20–25.

Fall Spice Liqueur

Use this liqueur in hot cider (see the recipe below) and as an accompaniment to fresh pumpkin pie, or a fine finish to Thanksgiving dinner.

- ½ cup light brown sugar
- ½ cup white sugar
- 2¼ cups apple juice
- 1 teaspoon pure vanilla extract
- 1 cinnamon stick
- ½ teaspoon ground ginger
- ½ teaspoon ground nutmeg
- ½ teaspoon ground cloves
- ½ teaspoon ground allspice
- 1 cup brandy
- ½ cup 100-proof vodka

Bring brown sugar, white sugar, and apple juice to a boil over medium-high heat. Add vanilla, cinnamon, ginger, nutmeg, cloves, and allspice. Boil for 4 minutes; then remove from heat. Let stand until just warm. Use a fine-mesh strainer to strain out solids. Discard. Transfer liquid to a clean 1-quart container with a tight-fitting lid. Add brandy and vodka. Cover and let stand in a cool, dark place for 1 month.

Rack or filter liqueur into final container. Enjoy now or age for an additional month before serving. YIELD: APPROX. 1 QUART

Hot Toddy Punch

- ¼ cup sugar
- 4 cups apple cider
- 1 cup Fall Spice Liqueur

Combine sugar and cider in saucepan and heat until mixture begins to steam. Remove from heat and add Fall Spice Liqueur. Serve in mugs with a cinnamon stick swizzler. SERVES 4.

Mandarin Spice Liqueur

This liqueur contains the exotic flavors of Asia. If you're having a Chinese take-out dinner, make it special with this cordial.

  1 cup honey
  1 cup water
  1 tablepoon chopped gingerroot
  2 star anise flowers
  ½ teaspoon ground cloves
  1 cinnamon stick
1½ cups light rum
  1 tablespoon orange zest

Bring honey and water to a boil over medium-high heat. Boil for 2 to 3 minutes, skimming off any foam that rises to the surface. Add gingerroot, star anise, cloves, and cinnamon. Boil for 2 minutes more, then remove from heat. Let stand until just warm. Transfer to a clean 1-quart container. Add rum and orange zest. Cover and let stand in a cool, dark place for 1 month.

Use a fine-mesh strainer to strain out solids. Discard. Transfer liqueur to clean container, cover, and let stand for 1 week more. Rack or filter liqueur into final container and age for 1 month before serving. YIELD: APPROX. 1 FIFTH

Suggestions for Use
Mandarin Spice Liqueur is great by itself, zippy in tea, or a spicy addition to an Asian marinade.

Vanilla Liqueurs

Vanilla comes from the seedpod of a tropical orchid indigenous to South America. Americans are most familiar with this spice in the form of vanilla extract, which is made either from synthetic vanilla or by macerating vanilla pods to make an alcoholic pure vanilla extract.

The flavor of vanilla is warm and inviting, the aroma comforting and cordial. The Aztecs used this now widely available spice to flavor chocolate drinks. In liqueurs, "plain" vanilla takes on a whole new meaning.

Vanilla Liqueur

½ cup light brown sugar, firmly packed
½ cup water
1 cup light corn syrup
3 tablespoons pure vanilla extract
1 cup 100-proof vodka
½ cup brandy

Bring brown sugar and water to a boil over medium-high heat, stirring constantly to prevent scorching. When clear, stir in corn syrup and heat for 1 minute more. Remove from heat and let stand until just warm. Transfer to a clean 1-quart container. Add vanilla, vodka, and brandy. Cover and let stand in a cool, dark place for 1 month before serving. YIELD: APPROX. 1 FIFTH

Vanilla Bean Liqueur

1½ cups sugar
1 cup water
2 whole vanilla beans
1 teaspoon glycerin (optional)
1½ cups 80-proof vodka

Bring sugar and water to a boil over medium-high heat, stirring constantly to prevent scorching. When clear, cool and pour into a clean 1-quart container. Add vanilla beans, glycerin (if using), and vodka. Cap container immediately to prevent evaporation of alcohol. With a little luck, sugar crystals should form on the vanilla beans. If crystals fail to form, no harm has been done; Vanilla Liqueur will still taste wonderful, and the bean in the bottle will still be decorative.

Let stand in a cool, dark place for at least 1 month. This liqueur is best presented in a clear glass container so that the vanilla beans are visible. YIELD: APPROX. 1 FIFTH

Locating Vanilla Beans
Vanilla beans are available in better grocery stores and gourmet shops.

CHAPTER 5

THE CREAM OF THE CROP

ream-based cordials are the ultimate in homemade liqueurs. Rich and luxurious, they can be filled with fresh fruit flavors, suffused with chocolate or nuts, or redolent of spices. Deciding how to flavor these recipes was easy. Achieving the rich, creamy texture was more difficult. We wanted a base that tasted of fresh cream, had just the right amount of sweetness, and would keep in the refrigerator. And we wanted a base that could age long enough for the flavors to blend into a mellow, complex cordial.

After some experimentation, we arrived at a formula for a cream base that can be mixed in bulk and used to make most homemade cream liqueurs. Experiment on your own using this base. Try the recipes elsewhere in this book as flavoring agents for cream-based liqueurs.

Most of the recipes in this chapter specify 80-proof vodka, which makes the alcohol component more subtle in these delicate drinks.

Cream Base

> 1 can (14 ounces) sweetened condensed milk
> 1 can (12 ounces) evaporated milk
> 1 cup whipping cream
> 1 cup Simple Syrup (see page 6)
> ¼ teaspoon potassium sorbate (optional)*

Mix all ingredients together in sterile 2-quart container. Use in the following recipes where Cream Base is indicated.
YIELD: APPROX. 1 QUART

*Potassium sorbate will help stabilize the liqueur. It is available where wine-making supplies are sold or through mail-order catalogs. Dissolve potassium sorbate in heated Simple Syrup before mixing it with the other ingredients.

Chocolate, Coffee, and Cream

We can't think of a better combination for a liqueur than chocolate, coffee, and cream. After you have tried our recipe for Irish Cream, you may be inspired to come up with your own variations.

Irish Cream Liqueur

Recipes for Irish Cream seem to make the rounds every Christmas. We tried several, sampled some of the commercial Irish Creams, and then came up with our own version. We hope you like it as much as we do. It's wonderful added to coffee.

¼	cup light brown sugar
¼	cup water
½	teaspoon powdered instant coffee
2	tablespoons chocolate syrup
1	teaspoon coconut extract
1	teaspoon pure vanilla extract
½	teaspoon almond extract
2	eggs
2½	cups Cream Base
1	cup Irish whiskey or brandy

Make a simple syrup by bringing brown sugar and water to a boil over medium-high heat, stirring constantly to prevent scorching. When clear, remove from heat and let stand until just warm. Dissolve coffee in warm syrup. Add chocolate syrup, coconut extract, vanilla, and almond extract. In separate bowl, beat eggs until frothy and fold into Cream Base. Add to syrup. Add whiskey or brandy and whisk to blend. Transfer to a sterile 1-quart container with tight-fitting lid. Cover and refrigerate immediately. Use within 2 weeks. YIELD: APPROX. 1 QUART

Health Caution

Since this version of Irish Cream contains uncooked eggs, make sure the eggs you choose are fresh and free of cracks.

Banana Cream

Making banana-flavored cream liqueurs requires excellent timing if you start with fresh fruit. Most bananas arrive in the supermarket wearing green jackets, ripen to golden yellow, and quickly develop brown spots, which makes them perfectly fit for banana bread but not for liqueurs. For cream liqueurs, you need perfectly ripe bananas — not too green, not too ripe, not bruised, and never, ever, stored in the refrigerator, where their flavorful sugars are quickly metabolized into starch. A more practical alternative is to use banana flavoring and let somebody else do the banana sitting.

- ½ cup sugar
- ½ cup water
- 2½ cups Cream Base
- 1 cup 80-proof vodka
- 1½ teaspoons concentrated banana flavoring extract
- ½ teaspoon pure vanilla extract
- 6 drops yellow food coloring

Make a simple syrup by bringing sugar and water to a boil over medium-high heat, stirring constantly to prevent scorching. When clear, remove from heat and let stand until just warm. Combine syrup, Cream Base, and vodka in sterile 1-quart container. Cover and shake to mix. Add flavoring, vanilla, and food coloring, cover, and shake again. Store in refrigerator for up to 1 month. YIELD: APPROX. 1 QUART

Fruits and Cream

There may be a fruit somewhere that isn't good in combination with cream, but we couldn't find one. We made fruit cream liqueurs with fresh fruit, flavoring oils, extracts, and syrups. Flavoring oils, extracts, and syrups have two advantages over fresh fruit. First, they are easier to use, and the quality of the finished liqueurs is comparable to that of liqueurs made with fresh fruits. Second, they are always "in season." That means you can make these cream liqueurs in the dead of winter — just in time to pour them into decorative bottles and give them as holiday gifts.

Chocolate-Covered Cherry Cream

This liqueur is a creamier, less cloying alternative to the classic chocolate-covered cherries that are popular holiday gifts. We guarantee that the doorman, cleaning person, mail carrier, and the rest of your service providers will enjoy it — and your services just may improve in anticipation of next year's homemade gift!

½ cup sugar
½ cup water
1 cup 80-proof vodka
½ cup maraschino cherry juice (juice from 10-ounce jar of cherries)
2 cups half-and-half
¾ teaspoon concentrated chocolate flavoring extract
1 teaspoon imitation almond extract
2 drops red food coloring

Make a simple syrup by bringing sugar and water to a boil over medium-high heat, stirring constantly to prevent scorching. When clear, remove from heat and let stand until just warm. Combine syrup and vodka in a sterile 1-quart container. Cover and shake to mix. Add cherry juice, half-and-half, chocolate flavoring, almond extract, and food coloring. Cover and shake until evenly colored. Store in refrigerator for up to 1 month.
YIELD: APPROX. 1 QUART

Variation: Maraschino Cherry Cream
Simply forgo the chocolate in the recipe above if you always thought the best part of a Shirley Temple is the cherry.

Coconut Cream

If you like your coconut straight, this is the liqueur for you.

- 1 cup sugar
- 1 cup water
- 1 can (14 ounces) coconut milk
- 2 teaspoons imitation coconut extract
- 1 cup 100-proof vodka

Make a simple syrup by bringing sugar and water to a boil over medium-high heat, stirring constantly to prevent scorching. When clear, remove from heat and let stand until just warm. Combine syrup, coconut milk, and coconut extract in a sterile 1-quart container. Mix thoroughly. Add vodka, cover, and stir or shake until blended. Store in refrigerator for up to 1 month.
YIELD: APPROX. 1 QUART

Coconut Milk?

Coconut milk isn't really milk. It's finely pureed coconut and is lighter than the other liquids in this recipe.

Coconut Liqueurs

You'll notice that our recipes for coconut liqueurs call for 100-proof vodka. That's because the coconut milk base stands up to the vodka better than does the Cream Base.

Also, because the liqueurs do not contain milk or milk products, you can store them for a longer period than you can liqueurs made with a cream or milk base. They do tend to separate, however, with the alcohol sinking to the bottom and the coconut floating to the top. Just shake vigorously before serving to disperse the coconut throughout the liqueur.

Pineapple-Coconut Cream

Rum, coconut, and pineapple are one eternal triangle that doesn't lead to trouble. If you're a skier, sledder, or shoveler, this liqueur is just the ticket to take off the chill after your winter-time outdoor activities.

1 cup sugar
1 cup water
1 can (14 ounces) coconut milk
1 teaspoon pure vanilla extract
2 teaspoons imitation coconut extract
1 cup Pineapple Rum (see chapter 8)

Make a simple syrup by bringing sugar and water to a boil over medium-high heat, stirring constantly to prevent scorching. When clear, remove from heat and let stand until just warm. Combine syrup, coconut milk, and vanilla and coconut extract in a sterile 1-quart container. Mix thoroughly. Add Pineapple Rum, cover, and stir or shake until blended. Store in refrigerator for up to 1 month. YIELD: APPROX. 1 QUART

Variation: *Strawberry-Coconut Cream*
Replace Pineapple Rum with 1 cup vodka and ¾ cup strawberry syrup for this strawberry-coconut treat.

Lemon Dream Cream

Even when it's coupled with cream, lemon's light and lively flavor keeps its zip and cleanses the palate. Try serving your guests the tiniest glass of Lemon Dream Cream between courses at your next Italian dinner and see how effectively it enhances the flavors that follow.

        ½ cup sugar
        ½ cup water
        1 cup Lemon Vodka (see chapter 8)
     2½ cups Cream Base
        ½ teaspoon pure vanilla extract
        2 teaspoons lemon extract
        6 drops yellow food coloring

Make a simple syrup by bringing sugar and water to a boil over medium-high heat, stirring constantly to prevent scorching. When clear, remove from heat and let stand until just warm. Combine syrup and Lemon Vodka in a sterile 1-quart container. Cover and shake to mix. Add Cream Base, vanilla, lemon extract, and food coloring. Cover and shake until evenly colored. Store in refrigerator for up to 1 month. YIELD: APPROX. 1 QUART

Lemon Dream Soda

Make this Lemon Dream Soda for a cool and refreshing summer sipper.

Fill half a tall glass with Lemon Dream Cream Liqueur, add a scoop of lemon-lime or lemon sherbet, and carefully add lemon-lime soda to fill. Top with a dollop of whipped cream and a cherry. For a colorful variation, use orange sherbet and top with a sprig of mint.

Serving Suggestion

Serve Mango Cream well chilled with a twist of lemon and a slice of cheesecake for a dessert you and your guests will want to linger over. Delicious!

You can find mangoes in the produce section of the supermarket, waiting patiently to ripen to the point where they lose their astringent flavor and hard texture. The ideal mango is slightly soft and has a rosy blush on smooth yellow-green skin. If the mango doesn't give when you squeeze it, it's not ripe. Buy it anyway. It will blush nicely in a fruit bowl and soften up after a few days at room temperature.

Mango Cream

If your taste tends toward the exotic, try this distinctive liqueur. Your friends may not know exactly what fruit they're tasting, but they'll be sure to ask for more. The blending of mango, cream, and spices makes this one of our most sophisticated recipes.

  1 cup ripe mango
  1 cup Spiced Rum (see chapter 8)
  ½ cup sugar
  ½ cup water
1½ cups Cream Base
  ½ teaspoon pure vanilla extract
  1 teaspoon lemon extract
  4 drops yellow food coloring
  2 drops red food coloring

Cut flesh away from pit of mango. Discard pit and puree fruit in blender. Transfer to covered container, add Spiced Rum, and macerate for 2 weeks, stirring frequently for maximum surface contact with the alcohol.

Use a fine-mesh strainer to strain out solids. Transfer liquid to a sterile 1-quart container. Make a simple syrup by bringing sugar and water to a boil over medium-high heat, stirring constantly to prevent scorching. When clear, remove from heat and let stand until just warm. Add syrup, Cream Base, vanilla and lemon extracts, and yellow and red food coloring to jar. Cover and stir or shake to blend. Refrigerate immediately and use within a few days. YIELD: APPROX. 1 QUART

Brandy-Orange Cream

A little like a sophisticated eggnog, this cordial is sure to be a hit at your holiday party. The combination of orange, spices, and cream is subtle and smooth, with just enough sweetness to make it sing. The spices stay suspended in the Cream Base, so you don't need to strain them out.

    ½ cup sugar
    ½ cup water
     1 cup brandy
    ¼ teaspoon orange flavoring oil
    ½ teaspoon pure vanilla extract
   2½ cups Cream Base
    ¼ teaspoon ground cinnamon
    ¼ teaspoon ground cloves

Make a simple syrup by bringing sugar and water to a boil over medium-high heat, stirring constantly to prevent scorching. When clear, remove from heat and let stand until just warm. Combine syrup, brandy, and flavorings in a sterile 1-quart container. Add Cream Base, cinnamon, and cloves. Cover and shake until thoroughly mixed. Refrigerate immediately and age for 1 week before serving. Store for up to 1 month.
YIELD: APPROX. 1 QUART

Orange Liqueurs

Visit a region where oranges are grown, and you'll realize that there are as many varieties of oranges as there are of apples. Each variety may have a slightly different flavor or degree of sweetness. Commercial orange flavorings are more consistent, but they do vary from company to company.

Suggestions for Use

Add some Brandy-Orange Cream Liqueur to freshly brewed coffee or a strong cup of tea for a perfect nightcap.

Dreamsicle Liqueur

Remember when you were a kid and went to the corner store for a Creamsicle on a hot summer day? You can capture some of that magic with this recipe.

½ cup sugar
½ cup water
1½ cups 80-proof vodka
¼ teaspoon sweet orange flavoring oil
2 teaspoons pure vanilla extract
½ cup condensed orange juice*
1 can (14 ounces) sweetened condensed milk
4 drops red food coloring
6 drops yellow food coloring

Make a simple syrup by bringing sugar and ½ cup water to a boil over medium-high heat, stirring constantly to prevent scorching. When clear, remove from heat and let stand until just warm. Combine vodka and flavorings in sterile 1-quart container. Add syrup, condensed orange juice, and condensed milk. Add yellow and red food coloring, adjusting the amount if necessary to achieve a creamy orange color. Cover and shake vigorously. Store in refrigerator for up to 1 month. YIELD: APPROX. 1 QUART

Variation: If you'd like a slushier version of this liqueur, pour it into an ice cube tray without the dividers, freeze for 1 to 3 hours, and spoon into footed sundae cups. It makes a wonderfully light dessert served with almond cookies or ladyfingers.

Condensed Juice

*Condensed orange juice is made using 1 can frozen orange juice concentrate and 2 cans water.

Peaches and Cream  QUICK & EASY

You won't need to worry about serving dessert if you make this liqueur your meal's finale. We first made it with fresh peaches macerated in vodka for 2 to 3 weeks. We strained out the fruit, then proceeded as in the following recipe, adding the peach-flavored vodka to the Cream Base and the remaining ingredients. You can make your cordial that way if peaches are plentiful and if you have the time. When we tried the recipe using the peach flavoring extract, however, we were able to produce the same creamy peach flavor with a lot less work. Quick and easy doesn't mean inferior quality in these cordials.

½	cup sugar
½	cup water
2½	cups Cream Base
1	cup 80-proof vodka
3	teaspoons concentrated peach flavoring extract
½	teaspoon pure vanilla extract
6	drops yellow food coloring
2	drops red food coloring

Make a simple syrup by bringing sugar and water to a boil over medium-high heat, stirring constantly to prevent scorching. When clear, remove from heat and let stand until just warm. Combine syrup, Cream Base, and vodka in a clean 1-quart container. Add flavorings, cover, and shake to mix. Add yellow and red food coloring and shake again until evenly colored. Cover and store in refrigerator for up to 1 month.

YIELD: APPROX. 1 QUART

A Wonderful Smell
Peaches and Cream Liqueur smells heavenly. For that reason, we like to serve it in wide-mouthed wineglasses to take full advantage of the delectable aroma.

Picnic on the Beach

Pack this beach snack for you and your favorite companion. Line two kiddie beach buckets with colorful napkins. Add to each a small bottle of Raspberry Cream Cordial; a baby food jar filled with brown sugar; another jar filled with sour cream; a small tub of softened cream cheese blended with a tablespoon of Raspberry Cream Cordial and chopped walnuts; small, crispy rice crackers; and a container of fresh raspberries. Tuck a seafood fork, canapé knife, and cordial glass into each bucket. Then enjoy your repast like this: Spread cream cheese on crackers and nibble as you sip Raspberry Cream Cordial. For dessert, spear each raspberry with the tiny fork and dip it first into sour cream and then into brown sugar. Finish with a second serving of Raspberry Cream Cordial.

Raspberry Cream

We've never met a raspberry we didn't like. If you've made the Raspberry Liqueur in chapter 2, you'll understand why. If you haven't tried that recipe yet, we suggest that you do so — but make a double batch. One batch will be for sipping, the other for this sinfully rich cream liqueur.

½ cup sugar
½ cup water
1 cup Raspberry Liqueur (see chapter 2)
½ cup brandy
½ teaspoon lemon extract
2 cups Cream Base

Make a simple syrup by bringing sugar and water to a boil over medium-high heat, stirring constantly to prevent scorching. When clear, remove from heat and let stand until just warm. Combine syrup, Raspberry Liqueur, brandy, and lemon extract in a sterile 1-quart container. Cover and shake to mix. Add Cream Base, cover, and shake again. Store in refrigerator for up to 1 month. YIELD: APPROX. 1 QUART

Strawberries and Cream

If someone had told us that a liqueur this delicious could be made this easily with strawberry syrup, we wouldn't have believed him. If you want to make Strawberries and Cream with fresh strawberries, you can do it by macerating sliced strawberries in vodka, straining them out, and adding the flavored vodka to the remaining ingredients. That works great in June. For the rest of the year, you'll get equally lovely results with flavored syrups.

½ cup sugar
½ cup water
2½ cups Cream Base
2 teaspoons strawberry extract
1 cup 80-proof vodka
¾ cup strawberry syrup
2 drops red food coloring

Make a simple syrup by bringing sugar and water to a boil over medium-high heat, stirring constantly to prevent scorching. When clear, remove from heat and let stand until just warm. Combine syrup, Cream Base, vodka, and strawberry extract in a sterile 1-quart container. Add strawberry syrup and food coloring, cover, and shake to mix. Store in refrigerator for up to 1 month.

YIELD: APPROX. 1 QUART

Delicious Desserts

This liqueur makes wonderful parfaits — pretty, pink, and practically effortless. Or try it over sponge cake for an easy — but sophisticated — dessert.

Nuts and Cream

Nuts and cream make a delight-ful combination, and if you use the flavorings and syrups we recommend, creamy nut cor-dials are among the easiest and most delicious liqueurs you can make. We usually have at least one of these nutty cordials in the refrigerator because they make tasty additions to coffee at the end of a meal. They are mellow and mild and comple-ment most desserts — from elegant tortes to simple sugar cookies.

Creamy Almond Delight

If you are one of those folks who think a little almond goes a long way, you may want to experiment to see just how much almond flavoring to add to this liqueur. Start out with half the amount suggested and add more until you've created the perfect cordial for your taste.

½	cup sugar
½	cup water
1	cup brandy
1½	teaspoons almond flavoring oil
½	teaspoon pure vanilla extract
2½	cups Cream Base

Make a simple syrup by bringing sugar and water to a boil over medium-high heat, stirring constantly to prevent scorching. When clear, remove from heat and let stand until just warm. Combine syrup, brandy, and vanilla and almond flavoring in a sterile 1-quart container. Add Cream Base, cover, and shake until well mixed. Store in refrigerator for up to 1 month.

YIELD: APPROX. 1 QUART

Pousse-Café

Creamy Almond Delight is a wonderful ingredient for a pousse-café, which is made from different liqueurs poured carefully into a glass so that one floats on top of the other.

Pour ½ glass Crème de Cacao, then ½ glass Creamy Almond Delight over the back of a spoon to keep the liqueurs separate.

Sip and enjoy.

Chocolate-Hazelnut Cream

Think about the most delicious chocolate you've ever tasted — smooth, rich, creamy, and wickedly decadent. Then imagine that it is laced with hazelnuts. If that sounds like heaven to you, just wait until you taste this liqueur. Nobody turns down seconds!

1	cup brandy
½	cup hazelnut syrup
3	tablespoons chocolate syrup
1	teaspoon pure vanilla extract
2½	cups Cream Base

Combine brandy, hazelnut syrup, chocolate syrup, and vanilla in a sterile 1-quart container. Add Cream Base, cover, and shake until well mixed. Store in the refrigerator for up to 1 month.
YIELD: APPROX. 1 QUART

Chocolate Creativity

Find the tiniest containers to fill with Chocolate Hazelnut Cream Liqueur, then replace some of the candy in a box of chocolates with them. You'll satisfy your sweetie's sweet tooth and create a creative impression at the same time. You may need to store this gift in the refrigerator, but *you'll* get a warm reception.

Butter Pecan Cream Cordial

Butter pecan is always one of the flavors available at specialty ice cream shops. Butter Pecan Cream Cordial has all the appeal of the ice cream, but with a kick.

½ cup sugar
½ cup water
1 cup 100-proof vodka
3 teaspoons concentrated butter pecan
flavoring extract
½ teaspoon pure vanilla extract
2½ cups Cream Base

Make a simple syrup by bringing sugar and water to a boil over medium-high heat, stirring constantly to prevent scorching. When clear, remove from heat and let stand until just warm. Combine vodka and flavorings in sterile 1-quart container. Add Cream Base and syrup and shake until well mixed. Store in refrigerator for up to 1 month. YIELD: APPROX. 1 QUART

Pralines and Cream Cordial

At a recent family gathering of 20 people, we took a little ribbing about the quart jars of multicolored cream liqueurs that filled one shelf of the refrigerator. Of course, everyone wanted to taste them. When our guests had gone, the Pralines and Cream jar was almost empty. Delicious alone or as an addition to coffee, it won't last much longer in your house than it did in ours!

Any liqueur on these pages is a welcome addition to a number of dessert recipes, including this easy cheese cake, below.

½	cup light brown sugar
½	cup water
1	cup brandy
1½	teaspoons concentrated praline flavoring oil
½	teaspoon pure vanilla extract
2½	cups Cream Base

Make a simple syrup by bringing brown sugar and water to a boil over medium-high heat, stirring constantly to prevent scorching. When clear, remove from heat and let stand until just warm. Combine brandy and flavorings in a sterile 1-quart container. Add Cream Base and syrup, cover, and shake until well mixed. Store in refrigerator for up to 1 month. YIELD: APPROX. 1 QUART

Pecan Cheesecake

¼	cup Creamy Pecan Cordial
8	ounces cream cheese, softened
¼	cup orange juice
2	cups whipped dessert topping
1	prepared graham cracker crust
	Caramel ice cream topping to taste
	Chopped toasted pecans

Combine cordial and cream cheese by hand. Blend in orange juice using electric mixer. Blend in whipped topping and pour mixture into crust. Refrigerate until firm. Drizzle ice cream topping over cheesecake and sprinkle with pecans.

CHAPTER 6

CANDY CORDIALS

Many chefs say that a taste of something sweet at the end of a meal signals your brain that it's time to stop. These candy cordials serve that purpose. They are sweet and delicious, and a small amount seems to put a ribbon around your meal. They may even be acceptable for dieters, since candy cordials are consumed in such small amounts.

Most of our candy cordials are made with commercial flavorings. The recipes vary only slightly, making it easy to substitute other flavors. When we first made some of our cordials, we thought they might be rather odd. Pink Bubble Gum, for example, elicited an "Are you kidding?" from at least one member of our team. We've included in this chapter full recipes for only some of our favorites, but encourage you to try a few of the following flavor substitutions: Maplenut Goodie, Bubble Gum, Cotton Candy, Chocolate Coconut, and Red Licorice. Have fun.

101

Butterscotch Liqueur

Reminiscent of a flavored schnapps called ButterShots, this liqueur is delicious by itself, but we prefer it in tea, coffee, or hot chocolate. Because it blends so well with hot drinks, Butterscotch Liqueur brings a warm and friendly end to winter suppers, whether you serve it with coffee or pour it over warm bread pudding.

       1 cup sugar
       1 cup water
    ½ cup brandy
       1 cup 100-proof vodka
    1½ teaspoons concentrated butterscotch flavoring extract
    10 drops yellow food coloring

Make a simple syrup by bringing sugar and water to a boil over medium-high heat, stirring constantly to prevent scorching. When clear, remove from heat and let stand until just warm. Pour into a clean 1-quart container and add brandy, vodka, flavoring, and food coloring. Cover and shake vigorously to blend. Let stand in a cool, dark place for 1 month before serving. YIELD: APPROX. 1 QUART

Caramel Liqueur

This liqueur isn't chewy, but it does have that rich caramel flavor that so many people love. If you're a fan of nutty caramels, you can add toasted walnut or pecan flavoring to this liqueur.

- 2 cups sugar
- 2 cups water
- 1½ teaspoons concentrated caramel flavoring extract
- ¾ cup brandy
- ¾ cup 100-proof vodka
- 4 drops caramel food coloring

Make a simple syrup by bringing sugar and water to a boil over medium-high heat, stirring constantly to prevent scorching. When clear, remove from heat and let stand until just warm. Pour into a clean 1-quart container and add brandy, vodka, flavoring, and coloring. Cover and shake vigorously to blend. Let stand in a cool, dark place for 1 month before serving.
YIELD: APPROX. 1 QUART

Serving Suggestions

Caramel Liqueur is a lovely cordial to serve with coffee and cream. Try it also as a topping for your favorite ice cream, or with fresh-baked apple pie.

Chocolate Liqueur

Some researchers say that chocolate produces some of the same chemicals in our bodies as does being in love. Chocolate lovers knew that already! Combine the sensuous chocolate flavoring with brandy, and this seductive liqueur is sure to sweep you off your feet.

2	cups sugar
2	cups water
1½	teaspoons concentrated chocolate flavoring extract
¾	cup brandy
¾	cup 100-proof vodka
4	drops caramel food coloring

Make a simple syrup by bringing sugar and water to a boil over medium-high heat, stirring constantly to prevent scorching. When clear, remove from heat and let stand until just warm. Pour into a clean 1-quart container and add brandy, vodka, flavoring, and coloring. Cover and shake vigorously to blend. Let stand in a cool, dark place for 1 month before serving.
YIELD: APPROX. 1 QUART

English Toffee Liqueur

Did you ever wish you could eat delicious English toffee without having it stick to your teeth? Now you can. This liqueur has the same rich flavor combined with the warmth of brandy — a perfect way to satisfy your sweet tooth.

    2 cups sugar
    2 cups water
 1½ teaspoons concentrated English toffee flavoring
       extract
    ¾ cup brandy
    ¾ cup 100-proof vodka
    4 drops caramel food coloring

Make a simple syrup by bringing sugar and water to a boil over medium-high heat, stirring constantly to prevent scorching. Pour into a clean 1-quart container and add brandy, vodka, flavoring, and food coloring. Cover and shake vigorously to blend. Let stand in a cool, dark place for 1 month before serving.
YIELD: APPROX. 1 QUART

Honey Liqueur

Honey lovers will find this cordial deliciously different from the usual candy cordials. You can vary the taste by choosing different kinds of honey, such as clover, orange blossom, or sage.

1¼ cups sugar
1¼ cups water
1¼ cups honey
1¼ cups brandy

Make a simple syrup by bringing sugar and water to a boil over medium-high heat, stirring constantly to prevent scorching. When clear, remove from heat and let stand until just warm. Combine syrup, honey, and brandy in a clean 1-quart container. Cover and shake vigorously to blend. This will produce foam on the top as traces of beeswax present in the honey are released. Skim off foam and discard. Cover and let stand in a cool, dark place for 1 month before serving. YIELD: APPROX. 1 QUART

A Versatile Liqueur

We always keep Honey Liqueur on hand because, in addition to being so delicious, it enlivens many other drinks. It's lovely in a wide variety of hot teas, and a perfect addition to sun tea in summer, served with a sprig of mint or a cinnamon swizzler. Not a tea drinker? Try Honey Liqueur in coffee.

Peppermint Pattie

Cool and chocolatey, this cordial will remind you of those delicious little two-tone mints that restaurants sometimes pass out with the check — to put you in a better mood, no doubt. If you make this cordial, you can improve your mood without picking up the tab.

- 1 cup sugar
- 1 cup water
- 1½ cups 100-proof vodka
- ½ cup brandy
- 1½ teaspoons concentrated chocolate flavoring extract
- ¾ teaspoon peppermint flavoring oil

Make a simple syrup by bringing sugar and water to a boil over medium-high heat, stirring constantly to prevent scorching. When clear, remove from heat and let stand until just warm. Pour into a clean 1-quart container and add vodka, brandy, peppermint flavoring, and chocolate flavoring. Cover and shake vigorously to blend. Let stand in a cool, dark place for 1 month before serving. YIELD: APPROX. 1 QUART

Wintergreen Liqueur

- 1¼ cups sugar
- 1½ cups water
- 1½ cups 100-proof vodka
- ¾ teaspoon wintergreen flavoring oil
- 3 drops red food coloring

Make a simple syrup by bringing sugar and water to a boil over medium-high heat, stirring constantly to prevent scorching. When clear, remove from heat and let stand until just warm. Pour into a clean 1-quart container and add vodka, flavoring, and food coloring. Cover and shake vigorously to blend. Let stand in a cool, dark place for 1 month before serving.
YIELD: APPROX. 1 QUART

Orange Truffle Liqueur

Some folks — who probably wish to remain anonymous — like to squeeze the chocolates in a box to find the truffles. They may not agree on just which kind is best, but they do agree that the truffles are worth squeezing for. This cordial is one of the luscious ones.

    1 cup sugar
    1 cup water
   1½ cups 100-proof vodka
    ¾ teaspoon orange flavoring oil
    ¾ teaspoon concentrated chocolate flavoring
       extract

Make a simple syrup by bringing sugar and water to a boil over medium-high heat, stirring constantly to prevent scorching. When clear, remove from heat and let stand until just warm. Pour into a clean 1-quart container and add the vodka, orange flavoring, and chocolate flavoring. Cover and shake vigorously to blend. Let stand in a cool, dark place for 1 month before serving. YIELD: APPROX. 1 QUART

Variation: *Rum Truffle Liqueur brings the added flavor of rum to the equation. Just add 1½ cups dark rum in place of the vodka.*

Red Licorice Liqueur

Okay, so red licorice isn't for everyone. But if you are one of those who still love the flavor, even though childhood has long since passed, you'll find this to be a very authentic red licorice treat.

- 1¼ cups sugar
- 1½ cups water
- 1¼ cups 100-proof vodka
- ¾ teaspoon concentrated red licorice flavoring extract
- 20 drops red food coloring (optional)

Make a simple syrup by bringing sugar and water to a boil over medium-high heat, stirring constantly to prevent scorching. When clear, remove from heat and let stand until just warm. Pour into a clean 1-quart container and add the vodka, red licorice flavoring, and, if you choose to use it, the food coloring. Cover and shake vigorously to blend. Let stand in a cool, dark place for 1 month before serving. YIELD: APPROX. 1 QUART

CHAPTER 7

COFFEE, ANYONE?

To a coffee lover, the fragrance of freshly brewed coffee fortifies the spirit and promises an energetic start to the day. But coffee also has a softer, warmer side when combined with spirits. Served alone, in a variety of mixed drinks, or in desserts, coffee liqueurs are at the top of our list of easy-to-make and enthusiastically received homemade cordials. Use our recipes for starters, then try substituting your favorite gourmet coffees for our choices. Here are a few other hints and suggestions:

◆ For best results, use freshly brewed coffee made from beans you grind yourself.
◆ Do not boil the coffee with the syrup mixture. Boiling coffee releases bitter oils, which may detract from the rich coffee flavor of the liqueur.
◆ Alcohol evaporates at a lower temperature than water, so adding it before the mixture has cooled will cause some of the alcohol to evaporate.
◆ Glycerin gives the liqueur its characteristic body — a little thicker than the vodka and brandy alone — but it may be omitted if you don't mind a thinner liqueur.
◆ You may find some sediment at the bottom of the container after your liqueur has aged. If you prefer a clearer liqueur, rack or filter into a clean container. If you have added glycerin, we recommend racking rather than filtering or adding glycerin at the very end once the liqueur is clear.

Amaretto Coffee Liqueur

2½ cups water, divided
6 tablespoons Colombian coffee
3 cups sugar
1 teaspoon pure vanilla extract
2½ cups 80-proof vodka
1 cup brandy
¾ teaspoon almond flavoring oil
1½ teaspoons glycerin (optional)

Combine 1½ cups water and coffee to make a very strong brew. Set aside. Make a simple syrup by bringing remaining 1 cup water and sugar to a boil over medium-high heat, stirring constantly to prevent scorching. When clear, remove from heat and let stand until just warm. Add vanilla and coffee. Combine vodka, brandy, flavoring, and glycerin (if using) in clean 2-quart container. Add coffee mixture. Cover and let stand in a cool, dark place for at least 1 month before serving. YIELD: APPROX. 1½ QUARTS

Café Maria Liqueur
(Our Version of Tía Maria)

We always think of Tía Maria as the Caribbean cousin of Kahlúa, since it's a rum-based liqueur typical of that region. The flavor is a little more subtle, and it is slightly sweeter than its Latin American cousins. Our version captures the warm, friendly flavors of the tropics.

2½	cups water, divided
6	tablespoons Jamaican coffee
1	cup white sugar
1	cup light brown sugar
1½	tablespoons pure vanilla extract
3	cups dark rum
1½	teaspoons glycerin (optional)

Combine 1½ cups water and coffee to make a very strong brew. Set aside. Make a simple syrup by bringing remaining 1 cup water, white sugar, and brown sugar to a boil over medium-high heat, stirring constantly to prevent scorching. When clear, remove from heat and let stand until just warm. Add vanilla and coffee. Mix rum and glycerin (if using) and combine all liquids in clean 2-quart container. Cover and let stand in a cool, dark place for at least 1 month before serving. YIELD: APPROX. 2 QUARTS

What's in a Name?
Tía Maria is Spanish for "Aunt Mary." Perhaps that homey image best identifies the character of this Caribbean liqueur.

Chocolate-Orange Coffee Liqueur

2½ cups water, divided
  6 tablespoons Colombian coffee
  3 cups sugar
  2 teaspoons pure vanilla extract
  ⅓ cup chocolate syrup
  3 tablespoons Orange Essence*
2½ cups 80-proof vodka
  1 cup brandy
1½ teaspoons glycerin (optional)

Combine 1½ cups water and coffee to make a very strong brew. Set aside. Make a simple syrup by bringing remaining 1 cup water and sugar to a boil over medium-high heat, stirring constantly to prevent scorching. When clear, remove from heat and let stand until just warm. Combine with remaining ingredients in clean 2-quart container. Cover and let stand in a cool, dark place for at least 1 month before serving.

   You may find some sediment at the bottom of the container. If you would prefer a clearer liqueur, rack or filter into a clean container. If you have added glycerin, we recommend racking rather than filtering. YIELD: APPROX. 1½ QUARTS

Making Orange Essence

*To make Orange Essence, use a vegetable peeler or zester to remove just the outer peel of a large orange. (The white inner peel will make the essence bitter.) Combine the zest (about ½ cup) with 1 cup grain alcohol or 100-proof vodka. Cover and let stand in a cool, dark place for 1 week. Strain out zest through fine-mesh strainer. Store covered in clean container.

Cinnamon Coffee Liqueur

If you love Mexican coffee, rich with the flavors of cinnamon and whipped cream, you'll love this liqueur. It's mostly coffee with just a hint of cinnamon.

2½ cups water, divided
6 tablespoons Colombian coffee
3 cups sugar
2 cinnamon sticks
1 teaspoon pure vanilla extract
2½ cups 80-proof vodka
1 cup brandy
1½ teaspoons glycerin (optional)

Serving Suggestion

You can serve Cinnamon Coffee Liqueur plain or fancy, but our preference is to add it to hot chocolate with a generous dollop of whipped cream.

Combine 1½ cups water and coffee to make a very strong brew. Set aside. Make a simple syrup by bringing remaining 1 cup water, sugar, and cinnamon sticks to a boil over medium-high heat, stirring constantly to prevent scorching. When clear, remove from heat and let stand until just warm. Add vanilla and coffee. Combine vodka, brandy, and glycerin (if using) in clean 2-quart container. Add coffee mixture. Cover and let stand in a cool, dark place for at least 1 month before serving, leaving cinnamon sticks in liqueur until ready to serve.
YIELD: APPROX. 1½ QUARTS

Flavoring

Most shops that sell gourmet coffees also have coffee flavorings. Use your favorites to make cordials you'll love to sip after dinner or with your favorite dessert.

Hazelnut Coffee Liqueur

We first ran into Italian hazelnut syrup in a little combination art gallery–coffee shop in a small college town in South Dakota. (That's a long way from Italy!) The coffee shop added the syrup to warm milk foamed in a cappuccino machine. The result was so delicious we bought a bottle of the syrup from the owner. We've tried it in a variety of liqueurs, and every one of them is delicious. Try adding this cordial to your cappuccino or to foamed milk.

2½	cups water, divided
6	tablespoons Colombian coffee
2½	cups sugar
1	teaspoon pure vanilla extract
2½	cups 80-proof vodka
1	cup brandy
½	cup hazelnut syrup
1½	teaspoons glycerin (optional)

Combine 1½ cups water and coffee to make a very strong brew. Set aside. Make a simple syrup by bringing remaining 1 cup of water and sugar to a boil over medium-high heat, stirring constantly to prevent scorching. When clear, remove from heat and let stand until just warm. Add vanilla and coffee. Combine vodka, brandy, hazelnut syrup, and glycerin (if using) in clean 2-quart container. Add coffee mixture. Cover and let stand in a cool, dark place for at least 1 month before serving.

YIELD: APPROX. 1½ QUARTS

Rico's South-of-the-Border Coffee Liqueur

This liqueur combines the two flavors — coffee and chocolate — so valued by the Maya Indians of Mexico and Guatemala. After a month or so of aging, this liqueur will transport you back to another time, where wealth was measured in chocolate and the aroma of roasting coffee wafted over Cobán's open market.

2½ cups water, divided
6 tablespoons freshly ground dark-roasted coffee
2 cups white sugar
1½ cups light brown sugar
1½ tablespoons pure vanilla extract
3 tablespoons chocolate syrup
2½ cups 80-proof vodka
1 cup brandy

Combine 1½ cups water and coffee to make a very strong brew. Set aside. Make a simple syrup by bringing remaining 1 cup water, white sugar, and brown sugar to a boil over medium-high heat, stirring constantly to prevent scorching. When clear, remove from heat and let stand until just warm. Add vanilla, chocolate syrup, and coffee. Combine vodka and brandy in clean 2-quart container. Add coffee mixture. Cover and let stand in a cool, dark place for at least 1 month before serving.

You may find some sediment at the bottom of the container. If you prefer a clearer liqueur, rack or filter into a clean container. YIELD: APPROX. 2 QUARTS

Prized Commodities

In the city of Cobán in the Guatemalan mountains, the aroma of roasting coffee beans mingles with the perfume of tropical flowers in the open market where the descendants of the Maya sell their wares. Visitors can buy the coffee beans still warm from the oven. Grown in the mountains surrounding the city, the coffee is so delicious that it is almost worth the trip to bring home a fresh supply.

The ancient Maya valued another local beverage even more highly than coffee. Chocolate was so important to them that it was the beverage of kings, and wealth was measured in cocoa beans.

A Perfect Present

Need a gift that will break the ice, but not the bank? Find a mug printed with just the right message. Add a sample-size envelope of pecan-flavored coffee and an airline-size bottle of Southern Pecan Coffee Liqueur. Fill the remaining space with biscotti and use ribbon to tie a gift card — so your friend knows who was so creative — onto the handle.

Southern Pecan Coffee Liqueur

This beverage is as warm and wonderful as the Old South. Rich and aromatic, it's also easy to make. Vary the amount of pecan flavoring to make it as nutty as you like.

2½ cups water, divided
6 tablespoons Colombian coffee
1 cup white sugar
2 cups light brown sugar
1 teaspoon pure vanilla extract
2½ cups 80-proof vodka
1 cup brandy
1½ teaspoons concentrated pecan flavoring extract
1½ teaspoons glycerin (optional)

Combine 1½ cups water and coffee to make a very strong brew. Set aside. Make a simply syrup by bringing remaining 1 cup water, white sugar, and brown sugar to a boil over medium-high heat. Lower heat and stir frequently to prevent scorching. When clear, remove from heat and add vanilla and coffee. Let stand until just warm. Combine vodka, brandy, flavoring, and glycerin (if using) in clean 2-quart container. Add coffee mixture. Let stand in a cool, dark place for at least 1 month before serving.
YIELD: APPROX. 1½ QUARTS

Spiced Coffee Liqueur

A little mysterious, a little exotic, this liqueur is an adventure waiting to happen.

2½	cups water, divided
6	tablespoons freshly ground dark-roasted coffee
3	cups sugar
12	whole allspice, crushed
2	cinnamon sticks
½	teaspoon ground cloves
½	teaspoon ground nutmeg
4	teaspoons pure vanilla extract
2½	cups 80-proof vodka
1	cup brandy
1½	teaspoons glycerin (optional)

Combine 1½ cups water and coffee to make a very strong brew. Set aside. Tie allspice, cloves, nutmeg, and cinnamon loosely in clean cotton cloth. Make a simple syrup by bringing remaining 1 cup water, sugar, and spice packet to a boil over medium-high heat, stirring constantly to prevent scorching. When clear, remove from heat and let stand until just warm. Add vanilla and coffee. Combine vodka, brandy, and glycerin (if using) in clean 2-quart container. Add coffee mixture. Do not remove spice packet. Cover and let stand in a cool, dark place for at least 1 month before serving. YIELD: APPROX. 1½ QUARTS

Vanilla Coffee Liqueurs

Try a vanilla-coffee soda, made with either of the following two liqueurs, for a refreshing summertime drink. Place a scoop of vanilla or coffee ice cream in a tall glass. Add 1 ounce of vanilla-coffee liqueur and blend with the ice cream. Add sparkling water until the glass is half full, then add another scoop of ice cream. Top with whipped cream and a cherry.

Vanilla Butternut Coffee Liqueur

2½ cups water, divided
6 tablespoons Colombian coffee
3 cups sugar
1 teaspoon pure vanilla extract
2½ cups 80-proof vodka
1 cup brandy
1½ teaspoons concentrated butternut flavoring extract
1½ teaspoons glycerin (optional)

Combine 1½ cups water and coffee to make a very strong brew. Set aside. Make a simple syrup by bringing remaining 1 cup water and sugar to a boil over medium-high heat, stirring constantly to prevent scorching. When clear, remove from heat and let stand until just warm. Add vanilla and coffee. Combine vodka, brandy, flavoring, and glycerin (if using) in clean 2-quart container. Add coffee mixture. Cover and let stand in a cool, dark place for at least 1 month before serving.

YIELD: APPROX. 1½ QUARTS

French Vanilla Coffee Liqueur

Who says a cordial has to be complicated to be good? We make this liqueur frequently because it's so easy, and everyone who tastes it asks for more.

2½ cups water, divided
6 tablespoons Colombian coffee
3 cups sugar
5 teaspoons pure vanilla extract
2½ cups 80-proof vodka
1 cup brandy
1½ teaspoons glycerin (optional)

What We Recommend

This liqueur is great for sipping and scrumptious over vanilla ice cream. We've even been known to add it to butter frosting for a new twist on some ordinary desserts.

Combine 1½ cups water and coffee to make a very strong brew. Set aside. Make a simple syrup by bringing remaining 1 cup water and sugar to a boil over medium-high heat, stirring constantly to prevent scorching. When clear, remove from heat and let stand until just warm. Add vanilla and coffee. Combine vodka, brandy, and glycerin (if using) in clean 2-quart container. Add coffee mixture. Cover and let stand in a cool, dark place for at least 1 month before serving. YIELD: APPROX. 1½ QUARTS

CHAPTER 8

FLAVORED BRANDIES, RUMS, AND VODKAS

The distinction between other liqueurs and flavored brandies, rums, and vodkas may seem arbitrary since these bases also appear in some of the other liqueurs in this book. But as we developed and tested these recipes, we noticed that with some liqueurs, the flavor of the base contributed significantly to the taste of the final product. The resulting liqueurs are sophisticated and subtle. You can taste the apples in apple brandy, for example, but you know it's *brandy* you're sipping. Flavored rum retains the warmth of the tropics, and vodka's cool undertones hover beneath citrus and currant liqueurs.

Here are a few preparation hints for these flavored liquors:

◆ Cutting fruit into thin slices allows more of the surface to come into contact with the spirit during the aging process and results in a more intense flavor.

◆ Flavors blend better at cool, not cold, temperatures, and the alcohol retards spoilage.

◆ If you number brandies, rums, and vodkas among the essential spirits in your well-stocked bar, wait till you taste the liqueurs that you can make from them! And don't forget to share. Flavored brandies make excellent hostess or holiday gifts.

Brandy-Based Liqueurs

You don't have to use the most expensive brandies to create liqueurs that taste as if they had languished for years in the dusty wine cellar of some French château. But don't use cheap brandy, either. Taste the brandy you plan to use. Adding fruits, sugars, and other ingredients will enhance the flavor of the brandy, not cover it up.

Using the Fruit

Add the fruit from this and other brandy-based liqueur recipes to fruitcake or other recipes calling for brandied fruit.

Apple Brandy

Almost any variety of apples will work for this drink as long as they are fully ripe.

> 1 cup sugar
> 1 cup water
> 2½ pounds ripe apples, stemmed and washed
> 1 bottle (1 fifth) brandy
> 1 teaspoon fruit protector

Make a simple syrup by bringing sugar and water to a boil over medium-high heat, stirring constantly to prevent scorching. When clear, remove from heat and let stand until just warm. Quarter, core, and thinly slice apples. Combine apples, syrup, brandy, and fruit protector in clean 2-quart jar with screw-on lid. (Or divide ingredients between two 1-quart jars.) Cover and let stand in a cool, dark place for 1 month. Do not refrigerate.

Use a fine-mesh strainer to strain out solids, and discard or reserve them for another use. Filter liqueur into clean container(s). Cover and let stand for 1 day before racking or filtering into final container(s). Age for 1 to 3 months before serving. YIELD: APPROX. 1 QUART

Apricot Brandy

Apricot brandy is so delicious, and our stock lasts such a short time once guests have tasted it, that although we prefer the fresh approach, we are unwilling to forgo the fun of making it until apricots are in season. That's when we use the dried apricot variation.

1	cup sugar
1	cup water
1½	pounds fresh apricots, stemmed and washed
1	teaspoon fruit protector
1	bottle (1 fifth) brandy

Make a simple syrup by bringing sugar and water to a boil over medium-high heat, stirring constantly to prevent scorching. When clear, remove from heat and let stand until just warm. Cut apricots in half, remove pits, and thinly slice. Combine apricots, syrup, brandy, and fruit protector in clean 2-quart jar with screw-on lid. (Or divide ingredients between two 1-quart jars.) Cover and let stand in a cool, dark place for 1 month. Do not refrigerate.

Use fine-mesh strainer to strain out solids. Discard or reserve for another use. Filter liqueur into clean container(s). Cover and let stand for 1 day before racking or filtering into final container. Age for 1 to 3 months before serving. YIELD: APPROX. 1 QUART

Variation: Make Dried Apricot Brandy by substituting 1 pound dried apricots for fresh and adding ½ cup water when combining ingredients.

Recipe Adjustments

Drying fruits concentrates the flavor and sugars present. When you use dried fruits in place of fresh, you will usually need to add more water and use less fruit to achieve the same degree of flavoring.

Blackberry Brandy

If you use cruets to store your flavored brandies, make sure that the one you use for blackberry brandy is sparkling clear. The deep, rich color is almost as appealing as the exotic flavor.

- 1 cup sugar
- 1 cup water,
- 1 pound fresh blackberries, picked over and washed
- 1 bottle (1 fifth) brandy
- 1 teaspoon fruit protector

Make a simple syrup by bringing sugar and water to a boil over medium-high heat, stirring constantly to prevent scorching. When clear, remove from heat and let stand until just warm. Place blackberries in large bowl and crush with potato masher or wooden spoon. Add fruit protector and let stand for 2 hours. Divide blackberries, syrup, and brandy between two clean 1-quart jars. Cover and let stand in a cool, dark place for 1 month, shaking once a day to prevent clumping of fruit.

Use a fine-mesh strainer to strain out solids. Discard or reserve for another use. Filter liqueur into clean containers. Cover and let stand for 1 day before racking or filtering into final containers. Age for 1 to 3 months before serving.
YIELD: APPROX. 1 QUART

Variations: You can make other flavored brandies by substituting raspberries, boysenberries, or loganberries.

Spiced Blackberry Brandy

Serve this spicy liqueur slightly warmed after a midwinter skating party to take off the chill and bring a rosy blush to your guests' cheeks.

- 1 cup sugar
- 1 cup water
- 1 pound fresh blackberries, picked over and washed
- 1 teaspoon fruit protector
- 1 bottle (1 fifth) brandy
- ½ teaspoon whole cloves
- ½ teaspoon ground allspice
- 2 cinnamon sticks
- 1 teaspoon freshly grated nutmeg

Beat the Cold

Serve this cordial, with a variety of cheeses and nut breads, in front of a crackling fire. You may find that everyone will agree that winter isn't so bad after all.

Make a simple syrup by bringing sugar and water to a boil over medium-high heat, stirring constantly to prevent scorching. When clear, remove from heat and let stand until just warm. Place blackberries in large bowl and crush berries with potato masher or wooden spoon. Add fruit protector and let stand for 2 hours. Divide blackberries, syrup, brandy, cloves, allspice, nutmeg, and cinnamon between two clean 1-quart jars. Cover and let stand in a cool, dark place for 1 month, shaking a number of times to prevent clumping of fruit.

Use a fine-mesh strainer to strain out solids. Discard. Filter liqueur into clean containers. Cover and let stand for 1 day before racking or filtering into final containers. Age for 1 to 3 months before serving. YIELD: APPROX. 1 QUART

Cherry Brandy

If you like ripe red cherries, you'll love this cherry brandy. Being particularly fond of cherries, we couldn't wait to sample it. Even without the required aging time, it was smooth and delicious; aged, it was even more mellow and full bodied.

> 1 cup sugar
> 1 cup water
> 1½ pounds fresh red cherries, stemmed, picked over, and washed
> 1 teaspoon fruit protector
> 1 bottle (1 fifth) brandy

Make a simple syrup by bringing sugar and water to a boil over medium-high heat, stirring constantly to prevent scorching. When clear, remove from heat and let stand until just warm. Cut cherries in half and remove pits. Place cherries in large bowl and crush with potato masher or wooden spoon. Add fruit protector and let stand for 2 hours. Divide cherries, syrup, and brandy between two clean 1-quart jars. Cover and let stand in a cool, dark place for 1 month, shaking a number of times to prevent clumping of fruit.

Use a fine-mesh strainer to strain out solids. Discard or reserve them for another use. Filter liqueur into clean containers. Cover and let stand for 1 day before racking or filtering into final containers. Age for 1 to 3 months before serving.

YIELD: APPROX. 1 QUART

Orange Brandy
(Our Version of Grand Marnier)

For authentic flavor, use a good-quality cognac or French brandy in this recipe. Although all the ingredients are listed below, only the cognac (or brandy) and orange zest are used in the first phase. Make sure to use Seville (sour) oranges.

   3 cups cognac or French brandy
½ cup Seville orange zest
   1 cup sugar
   1 cup water
   1 teaspoon glycerin (optional)

Place cognac or brandy and orange zest in clean 1-quart jar. Let stand for 2 months, shaking occasionally.

Use a fine-mesh strainer to strain out solids. Discard. Transfer liquid to clean container and let stand for 1 day. Rack or filter into clean container. Make a simple syrup by bringing sugar and water to a boil over medium-high heat, stirring constantly to prevent scorching. When clear, remove from heat and let stand until just warm. Add syrup and glycerin (if using) to orange-flavored cognac. Transfer to final container, cover, and age for 3 months before serving. YIELD: APPROX. 1 QUART

A Seville Salad

Seville oranges are a bit sour served fresh, but if you combine them with sweetened flaked coconut, they make a luscious ambrosia.

Peach Brandy

The aroma alone is enough to sell you and your guests on this fruity brandy. The taste is pure distilled pleasure.

- 1 cup sugar
- 1 cup water
- 1½ pounds fresh peaches, stemmed and washed
- 1 bottle (1 fifth) brandy
- 1 teaspoon fruit protector

Make a simple syrup by bringing sugar and water to a boil over medium-high heat, stirring constantly to prevent scorching. When clear, remove from heat and let stand until just warm. Cut peaches in half, remove pits, and thinly slice. Combine peaches, syrup, brandy, and fruit protector in clean 2-quart jar with screw-on lid. (Or divide ingredients between two 1-quart jars.) Cover and let stand in a cool, dark place for 1 month. Do not refrigerate.

Use a fine-mesh strainer to strain out solids. Discard or reserve for another use. Filter liqueur into clean container(s). Cover and let stand for 1 day before racking or filtering into final containers. Age for 1 to 3 months before serving.

YIELD: APPROX. 1 QUART

Variation: Make Spiced Peach Brandy by adding 2 cinnamon sticks and 4 whole cloves to the liqueur before the first aging phase.

Pear Brandy

If you are among those who love the flavor but not the texture of pears, pear brandy is for you. This cordial offers delicious pear flavor; warm, rich brandy; and no grit!

1½ pounds fresh pears, stemmed and washed
1 cup sugar
1 cup water
1 bottle (1 fifth) brandy
1 teaspoon fruit protector

Make a simple syrup by bringing sugar and water to a boil over medium-high heat, stirring constantly to prevent scorching. When clear, remove from heat and let stand until just warm. Quarter, core, and thinly slice pears. Combine pears, syrup, brandy, and fruit protector in clean 2-quart jar with screw-on lid. (Or divide ingredients between two 1-quart jars.) Cover and let stand in a cool, dark place for 1 month. Do not refrigerate.

Use a fine-mesh strainer to strain out solids. Discard or reserve for another use. Filter liqueur into clean container(s), cover, and age for 1 to 3 months before serving.

YIELD: APPROX. 1 QUART

Perfect Pear Presentation

If you make your Pear Brandy in late summer or early fall, it will be golden and perfect for an autumn gift basket. Line a basket with a harvest-theme printed napkin. Add a bottle of Pear Brandy, some golden cheddar cheese wrapped in orange or yellow cellophane, an assortment of crackers wrapped and tied with ribbon, and for dessert — what else? — a perfect golden pear.

Rum-Based Liqueurs

You and your honey are lounging on the sandy beach of a Caribbean island at sunset. A cool, fragrant breeze caresses your sun-kissed skin. You reach for your drink, a blend of rum and tropical fruits . . .

We suggest using either light or white rum as a base for most of our rum-based liqueurs, since dark rum often overwhelms subtle flavors.

Banana Rum

1 large, just-ripe banana, peeled
2 teaspoons fruit protector
2½ cups light rum
1 cup sugar
1 cup water
1 teaspoon pure vanilla extract

Mash banana in large bowl and add fruit protector. Transfer to clean 2-quart jar with screw-on lid. (Or divide between two 1-quart jars.) Pour rum over banana. Use a wooden spoon to press banana under rum so it doesn't turn black. Cover and let stand in a cool, dark place for 2 to 3 weeks.

Use a fine-mesh strainer to strain out solids. Discard. Make a simple syrup by bringing sugar and water to a boil over medium-high heat, stirring constantly to prevent scorching. When clear, remove from heat and let stand until just warm. Filter liqueur into large bowl, repeating until it is clear. Add syrup and vanilla and stir with wooden spoon. Transfer to clean container, cover, and age for 1 month. If necessary, rack or filter liqueur into clean container until clear. (Banana-flavored rum is harder to clear than some other liqueurs.) Transfer to final container, cover, and age for 1 month before serving.
YIELD: APPROX. 1 QUART

Citrus Rum

This luscious blending of flavors will be an instant success at parties and family gatherings.

- 1 cup sugar
- 1 cup water
- 1 tablespoon lime zest
- 1 tablespoon lemon zest
- 1 tablespoon orange zest
- 2 cups light rum

Make a simple syrup by bringing sugar and water to a boil over medium-high heat, stirring constantly to prevent scorching. When clear, remove from heat and let stand until just warm. Combine syrup, lime zest, lemon zest, orange zest, and rum in clean 1-quart jar with screw-on lid. Cover and let stand in a cool, dark place for 1 month.

Use a fine-mesh strainer to strain out solids. Discard. Transfer liqueur to clean container, cover, and let stand for 1 week. Rack or filter liqueur into final container, cover, and age for 3 weeks before serving. YIELD: APPROX. 1 QUART

Perfect Blend

If you feel adventurous, try blending this citrus rum with Spiced Rum (see page 140). It's delicious!

Coconut Rum

1 cup water
1 cup sugar
2 tablespoons imitation coconut extract
2¼ cups white rum

Combine water, sugar, extract, and rum in clean 2-quart jar with screw-on lid. Cover and let stand for 1 month in a cool, dark place before serving. YIELD: APPROX. 1 QUART

Rich's Banana Royale

If you're an amateur bartender, you'll soon learn that Coconut Rum tastes wonderful just about any way you serve it. Here's one of our favorites.

Place the following ingredients into a blender:

2 shot glasses coconut milk
3 shot glasses pineapple juice
2 shot glasses Coconut Rum
1 shot glass cream or half-and-half
1 ripe banana
½ cup crushed ice

Blend for 30 seconds or until the mixture is smooth and creamy. Pour into a tumbler and top with grated coconut.

Lemon Rum

1 cup sugar
1 cup water
3 tablespoons lemon zest
1 tablespoon fresh-squeezed lemon juice
2 cups light rum

Make a simple syrup by bringing sugar and water to a boil over medium-high heat, stirring constantly to prevent scorching. When clear, remove from heat and let stand until just warm. Combine syrup, lemon zest, lemon juice, and rum in clean 1-quart jar with screw-on lid. Cover and let stand in a cool, dark place for 1 month.

Use a fine-mesh strainer to strain out solids. Discard. Transfer liqueur to a clean container, cover, and let stand for 1 week. Rack or filter liqueur into final container, cover, and age for 3 weeks before serving. YIELD: APPROX. 1 QUART

Variation: Make Lime Rum by substituting equal amounts of lime zest and lime juice for lemon zest and lemon juice.

A Citrus Secret

Lemons and limes will be juicier if you "cook" them in the microwave oven on high for about 30 seconds.

Ripe Fruit

The flesh of ripe mangoes is sweet and juicy. Avoid the unpleasant astringent taste of unripe fruit by using only mangoes that are rosy over yellow-green skins.

Mango Rum

Mangoes are one of our favorite tropical fruits. Great by themselves, they also make one of the tastiest salsas we've ever had. We could not pass up the opportunity to experiment with a liqueur based on this luscious fruit. Once you taste it, you'll never look at a mango in quite the same way again!

1 cup sugar
1 cup water
1 large mango
2 cups light rum
2 tablespoons honey
2 teaspoons fruit protector

Make a simple syrup by bringing sugar and water to a boil over medium-high heat, stirring constantly to prevent scorching. When clear, remove from heat and let stand until just warm. Thinly slice mango and divide evenly between two clean 1-quart jars. Divide syrup, rum, honey, and fruit protector between jars. Cover and let stand in a cool, dark place for 3 to 4 weeks.

Use a fine-mesh strainer to strain out solids. Crush solids to release juice and strain into liqueur. Discard solids. Transfer to clean container, cover, and let stand for 1 day before racking or filtering into final container. Age for 1 month before serving.
YIELD: APPROX. 1 QUART

Orange Rum

1 cup sugar
1 cup water
3 tablespoons orange zest
2½ cups light rum

Make a simple syrup by bringing sugar and water to a boil over medium-high heat, stirring constantly to prevent scorching. When clear, remove from heat and let stand until just warm. Combine syrup, orange zest, and rum in a clean 1-quart jar with a screw-on lid. Cover and let stand in a cool, dark place for 1 month.

Strain through fine mesh into clean jar. Discard solids. Cover and let stand for 1 week. Rack or filter into final container, cover, and age for 3 weeks before serving. YIELD: APPROX. 1 QUART

A Devilish Glaze

Orange Rum makes a delicious glaze for your favorite devil's food cake.

Orange Rum Glazed Cake

Bake devil's food cake according to your favorite recipe. While it's still warm, use the handle of a wooden spoon to make holes in the cake top, about 2 inches apart. Set aside while you prepare the following glaze.

1 cup sugar
¼ teaspoon cream of tartar
½ cup hot water
1 tablespoon Orange Rum
3 drops yellow food coloring
2 drops red food coloring
1 cup sifted powdered sugar

Cook sugar and water with cream of tartar over medium heat to make a thin syrup. Cool to lukewarm. Add Orange Rum and yellow and red food coloring. Stir in sifted powdered sugar until well blended. Pour glaze over cake and serve with a dollop of whipped cream.

Papaya Rum

Don't pass up this passionate fruit liqueur because papayas aren't your usual supermarket fare. Papaya-flavored rum is smooth, seductive, and sweetly reminiscent of a tropical vacation — and you don't even have to leave your easy chair.

- 1 cup sugar
- 1 cup water
- 3 cups ripe papaya, washed
- 3 cups light rum
- 2 tablespoons honey
- 2 teaspoons fruit protector

Make a simple syrup by bringing sugar and water to a boil over medium-high heat, stirring constantly to prevent scorching. When clear, remove from heat and let stand until just warm. Thinly slice papaya and divide evenly between two clean 1-quart jars. Divide syrup, rum, honey, and fruit protector between jars. Cover and let stand in a cool, dark place for 3 to 4 weeks.

Strain through fine mesh. Crush solids to release juice and strain into liqueur. Discard solids. Transfer liqueur to clean jar, cover, and let stand for 1 day before racking or filtering into final container. If needed, top off with rum and/or simple syrup to taste. Cover and age for 1 month. YIELD: APPROX. 1 QUART

Papaya Rum Smoothie

Place the following into a blender:

- ½ cup cubed fresh papaya
- ½ cup crushed ice
- 1½ shot glasses Papaya Rum
- 1 shot glass water

Blend for about 30 seconds, or until the mixture is smooth. Pour into a stemmed glass and decorate with a paper umbrella or garnish with an orange and a maraschino cherry.

Pineapple Rum

Pineapple juice and rum is a match made in heaven. You can use any part of the pineapple, including the core and outer portions that contain little bits of skin.

       3 cups sliced fresh, ripe pineapple
       1 cup light brown sugar
       1 cup pineapple juice
    2½ cups light or dark rum
       1 teaspoon fruit protector

Divide pineapple into two 1-quart jars. Mix brown sugar, pineapple juice, rum, and fruit protector. Add to jars. Cover and let stand in a cool, dark place for 3 to 4 weeks, shaking occasionally.

   Strain through fine mesh. Crush solids to release juice and strain into liqueur. Discard solids. Transfer liqueur to clean jar, cover, and let stand for 1 day before racking or filtering into final container. Cover and age for 1 month. YIELD: APPROX. 1 QUART

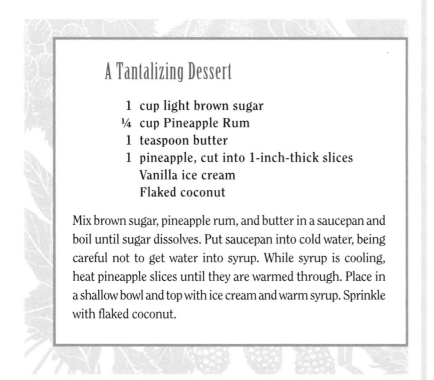

A Tantalizing Dessert

       1 cup light brown sugar
     ¼ cup Pineapple Rum
       1 teaspoon butter
       1 pineapple, cut into 1-inch-thick slices
          Vanilla ice cream
          Flaked coconut

Mix brown sugar, pineapple rum, and butter in a saucepan and boil until sugar dissolves. Put saucepan into cold water, being careful not to get water into syrup. While syrup is cooling, heat pineapple slices until they are warmed through. Place in a shallow bowl and top with ice cream and warm syrup. Sprinkle with flaked coconut.

Spiced Rum

We've always been big fans of spiced rum, perhaps because we live in the Midwest, where winters are very cold. There's nothing like a good mug of hot buttered rum to warm you up on a cold winter day.

Spiced Success

Our panel of taste-testers loved our Spiced Rum. We've had many not-too-subtle requests for a Christmas bottle, and we have to admit it's a great idea.

  1 cup sugar
  1 cup water
2½ cups dark rum
  4 teaspoons pure vanilla extract
12 whole allspice, crushed
  ½ teaspoon ground cloves
  ½ teaspoon ground nutmeg
  2 cinnamon sticks

Make a simple syrup by bringing sugar and water to a boil over medium-high heat, stirring constantly to prevent scorching. When clear, remove from heat and let stand until just warm. Combine syrup, rum, vanilla, allspice, cloves, nutmeg, and cinnamon in clean 1-quart jar with screw-on lid. Cover and let stand in a cool, dark place for 3 to 4 weeks.

Use a fine-mesh strainer to strain out solids. Discard. Transfer liqueur to clean container and serve immediately, or cover and age for 1 month more. Yield: Approx. 1 quart

Vanilla Rum

How can something so simple taste so good?

- 4 vanilla beans
- 2 cups dark rum
- 1 cup sugar
- 1 cup water
- 1 teaspoon glycerin (optional)

Place vanilla beans in clean 1-quart jar with screw-on lid and add rum. Cover and let stand in a cool, dark place for 2 to 3 weeks.

Use a fine-mesh strainer to strain out beans. Discard or reserve for another use. Transfer liquid to large bowl. Add syrup and glycerin (if using) to flavored rum. Pour into clean container, cover, and let stand for 1 to 2 months before serving.
YIELD: APPROX. 1 QUART

Vanilla Sugar

You can use the left-over vanilla beans to prepare vanilla sugar by nestling them in 2 cups sugar in a tightly closed container. The sugar is delicious in desserts, on cereal, or in tea or coffee. It's ready in about 2 weeks, but the flavor intensifies if you leave the beans in the sugar for a longer time.

Using Currants

You can reserve the currants for use in fruitcake or spice cakes or add them to your favorite poultry stuffing.

Currant Vodka

It's surprising how many of our guests who say they don't like currants and never drink vodka suddenly change their minds when we offer them a taste of Currant Vodka.

    1 cup sugar
    1 cup water
 1½ cups dried black currants
    3 cups 80-proof vodka
    1 teaspoon fruit protector

Make a simple syrup by bringing sugar and water to a boil over medium-high heat, stirring constantly to prevent scorching. When clear, remove from heat and let stand until just warm. Combine syrup, currants, vodka, and fruit protector in clean 2-quart jar. Cover and let stand in a cool, dark place for 2 months, shaking occasionally.

Use a fine-mesh strainer to strain out currants. Discard or reserve for another use. Filter liqueur into clean container. Cover and let stand for 1 day before racking or filtering into final container. Cover and age for 1 to 3 months before serving.
YIELD: APPROX. 1 QUART

Grapefruit Vodka

Try this liqueur in your salty dogs or our variation, below.

- 1½ cups sugar
- 1½ cups water
- ¼ cup grapefruit zest
- 3 cups 80-proof vodka
- 1 teaspoon fruit protector

Make a simple syrup by bringing sugar and water to a boil over medium-high heat, stirring constantly to prevent scorching. When clear, remove from heat and let stand until just warm. Combine syrup, grapefruit zest, vodka, and fruit protector in clean 2-quart jar with screw-on lid. (Or divide ingredients between two 1-quart jars.) Cover and let stand in a cool, dark place for 1 month.

Use a fine-mesh strainer to strain out solids. Discard. Transfer liqueur to clean container(s), cover, and let stand for 1 week. Rack or filter liqueur into final covered container(s) and age for 3 weeks before serving. YIELD: APPROX. 1 QUART

Flavored Vodkas

Vodka and citrus seem to complement each other naturally. Although vodka has little inherent taste, its composition brings out the cool citrus flavors. You may find yourself mixing your favorite vodka drinks with these elegant liqueurs.

Frothy Dog

This frothy concoction adds club soda to the standard salty dog.

Salt the rim of a collins or highball glass with sea salt. Then add the following:

- 1½ shot glasses grapefruit vodka
- 3 shot glasses grapefruit juice
- 1½ shot glasses club soda

Serve on the rocks and garnish with a wedge of lime.

Lemon Vodka

This is a cool, classy vodka, fine for sipping on the rocks or using in your favorite mixed drinks. We like to put it in the freezer before serving it as a summertime aperitif.

1 cup sugar
1 cup water
3 tablespoons lemon zest
1 tablespoon fresh-squeezed lemon juice
3 cups 80-proof vodka

Make a simple syrup by bringing sugar and water to a boil over medium-high heat, stirring constantly to prevent scorching. When clear, remove from heat and let stand until just warm. Combine syrup, lemon zest, lemon juice, and vodka in clean 2-quart jar. Cover and let stand in a cool, dark place for 1 month.

Use a fine-mesh strainer to strain out solids. Discard. Transfer liqueur to clean container(s), cover, and let stand for 1 week. Rack or filter liqueur into final container(s), cover, and age for 3 weeks before serving. YIELD: APPROX. 1 QUART

Variation: Make Lime Vodka by substituting equal amounts of lime zest and lime juice for lemon zest and lemon juice.

Orange Vodka

If you've already tried the recipe for Orange Brandy, you will have a very different experience with Orange Vodka. The two are as different as people born under the two March astrological signs — the cool but passionate Pisces (Orange Vodka) and the warm but aggressive Aries (Orange Brandy).

- 1 cup sugar
- 1 cup water
- 3 tablespoons orange zest
- 1 teaspoon fresh-squeezed lemon juice
- 3 cups 80-proof vodka

Make a simple syrup by bringing sugar and water to a boil over medium-high heat, stirring constantly to prevent scorching. When clear, remove from heat and let stand until just warm. Combine syrup, orange zest, lemon juice, and vodka in clean 2-quart jar. Cover and let stand in a cool, dark place for 1 month.

Use a fine-mesh strainer to strain out solids. Discard. Transfer liqueur to clean container(s), cover, and let stand for 1 week. Rack or filter liqueur into final container(s), cover, and age for 3 weeks before serving. YIELD: APPROX. 1 QUART

Orange Sour

Mixing drinks with liqueurs is a nifty way to bring new nuances to old favorites. Our Orange Sour is a little sweeter and smoother than the traditional vodka sour.

- 2½ ounces Orange Vodka
- 1 ounce fresh-squeezed lemon juice
- 1 teaspoon superfine sugar

Pour ingredients into a cocktail shaker with ice. Shake briskly, strain into a rocks glass, and garnish with a slice of orange and a maraschino cherry.

CHAPTER 9

SPIRITED FRUITS

Even more exotic than a finely crafted liqueur is a gift of fruits preserved in spirits. The visual effect is stunning and the taste of the fruit magical. One word of caution: Be careful to whom you give these gifts. Once your family and friends discover that you can make such tantalizing treats, you will be deluged with thinly veiled requests for them.

Alcohol-preserved fruits need to be fresh, free of blemishes, and generally at their peak. The alcohol will not camouflage an inferior fruit, only emphasize its poor quality.

Our favorite containers for fruits preserved in spirits are decorative jars with glass lids and wire closures. You also can use canning jars with two-piece lids or baby food jars. You can dress them up with a cap of printed cotton fabric tied around the neck with yarn.

Spirited fruits are especially tasty with meat dishes, but they also make a great accompaniment to casseroles and pasta dishes. Ordinary fare becomes something special when you serve fruits preserved in spirits.

We usually keep a jar or two in the refrigerator and add them to the menu when we have unexpected company. Sometimes our guests prefer a milder alcohol taste. If you do, too, heat the fruit before you serve it. The alcohol will evaporate, leaving just a hint of its tantalizing flavor behind. Spirited fruits are delicious served hot or cold.

Apricots in Cognac

4½ pounds fresh, ripe apricots
3 cups sugar
1½ cups honey
5 cups water
    Juice from ½ lemon
3 teaspoons orange zest
1 bottle (1 fifth) good-quality brandy or cognac

Inspect apricots to make sure you are using only the finest fruit. Wash with warm water, then pat dry. Using a medium-size sewing needle, make approximately 12 equally distributed pinpricks in the surface of each apricot. Bring sugar, honey, and water to a boil over medium-high heat. Skim off foam. Lower heat and stir frequently to prevent scorching. When clear, add apricots and continue cooking for 2 minutes more. Remove from heat and sprinkle with lemon juice. Cover and let stand for 8 to 12 hours or overnight.

Remove apricots from syrup and arrange in containers of your choice. Divide orange zest among containers, layering it between apricots for best effect. Bring syrup to a boil over medium-high heat, stirring frequently to prevent scorching. Boil for 5 minutes. Remove from heat and let cool for 1 hour. Combine syrup and brandy or cognac and pour over apricots. If necessary, top off with simple syrup. Cover tightly and let stand in a cool, dark place for 3 to 4 weeks before serving.

YIELD: APPROX. 2 GALLONS

Blueberry Bombs

2 cups fresh blueberries, picked over and washed
1 cup sugar
½ cup water
1 teaspoon lemon zest
   Juice from ½ lemon
1 cup 100-proof vodka
½ cup brandy

Place blueberries in clean 1-quart container and set aside. Make a simple syrup by bringing sugar and water to a boil over medium-high heat, stirring constantly to prevent scorching. When clear, remove from heat and let stand until just warm.

Add remaining ingredients and pour over blueberries. Cover and let stand 1 month before serving. YIELD: APPROX. 5 PINTS

Depth-Charged Fruit Salad

⅔ fifth bottle Lemon Vodka
½ cup superfine sugar
2 tablespoons lemon zest
1 watermelon
1 cantaloupe
1 honeydew melon
1 quart strawberries, hulled and washed
2 cups fresh pineapple chunks
1 pint Blueberry Bombs

Combine Lemon Vodka, sugar, and lemon zest and set aside. Cut watermelon in half lengthwise. Scoop out fruit and place in a large bowl along with any juice. Put rind in freezer. Scoop out cantaloupe and honeydew. Add to watermelon balls. Add strawberries, pineapple, and Blueberry Bombs; pour the vodka mixture over all and refrigerate.

To serve, fill the watermelon rind with the marinated fruit.

Stuffing Instructions

To stuff a fillet steak: Use a sharp knife to slice halfway through fillet as though cutting it into two thinner steaks. Fill middle with fruit and use toothpicks to skewer fillet back together.

Cherries with Spiced Rum

Versatility is the key to this recipe. You can use it to top ice cream or cheesecake or as sauce for ham and other meats. For something really special, stuff some of the spiced cherries into a split filet mignon, then reduce the liquid to make a classy sauce.

> 2 cups sugar
> 1 cup water
> 2 cups fresh dark, sweet cherries, washed and pitted
> 1½ cups Spiced Rum (see chapter 8, page 140)

Bring sugar and water to a boil over medium-high heat, stirring constantly to prevent scorching. When clear, add cherries and continue cooking for 2 minutes more. Remove from heat and let cool for about 10 minutes. Transfer to a clean 2-quart container and add the Spiced Rum. Cover tightly in a cool, dark place and let stand for 2 to 3 weeks before serving. YIELD: APPROX. 1½ QUARTS

Brandied Cranberry Relish

This relish makes a perfect gift for the hosts of your Thanksgiving feast. It's good as is, or you can heat it to remove the alcohol while retaining the flavor. Another great variation is to add a cup of coarsely chopped fresh cranberries and ½ cup sugar. This variation makes a wonderful accompaniment to roast turkey, chicken, or pork. Use it to smother the meat or serve it as a garnish with candied orange peel and a sprig of fresh mint at serving time.

  1 cup dried sweetened cranberries, loosely packed and divided
  ⅓ cup finely diced dried apricots, firmly packed
  ½ cup sugar
  ½ cup dry red wine
  ¾ cup water
  2 teaspoons orange zest
  1½ cups brandy

Combine ½ cup cranberries, apricots, sugar, wine, and water in saucepan. Bring to a boil over medum-high heat, reduce heat, and simmer for 5 minutes. Remove from heat and let cool for about 10 minutes. Transfer to clean 1-quart container. Add orange zest, brandy, and remaining ½ cup cranberries. Cover tightly and shake. Let stand in a cool, dark place for 2 to 3 weeks before serving. YIELD: APPROX. 1 QUART

Serving Suggestions

These figs make a fine light dessert served with a variety of cheeses, walnuts, and some Toasted Walnut Liqueur.

Fresh Figs in Honey Liqueur

This elegant treat reminds us of Indian summer — rich, golden, and gone too soon.

> 2 cups fresh figs, picked over and washed
> 1 teaspoon lemon zest
> 2 tablespoons fresh-squeezed lemon juice
> 1 cup honey
> 1 cup Honey Liqueur (see chapter 6, page 106)
> ½ cup cognac or brandy

Cut figs in half and layer in clean 1½-quart container. Divide lemon zest and lemon juice among layers, adding a little honey to each layer. Combine remaining honey, Honey Liqueur, and cognac or brandy in small bowl. Pour over figs. Cover and let stand in a cool, dark place for at least 3 weeks before serving.
YIELD: APPROX. 1½ QUARTS

Caribbean Fruit Salad in Rum Sauce

This is a fun gift for the host of a summer barbecue. Delicious served by itself, it also makes a great accompaniment to pork dishes.

¾ cup sliced fresh pineapple
¾ cup sliced fresh, ripe papaya
½ cup coarsely grated fresh coconut
¼ cup maraschino cherries, cut in half
½ cup mandarin orange slices
½ cup light brown sugar
2 tablespoons fresh-squeezed lemon juice
½ cup Vanilla Rum (see chapter 8, page 141)
½ cup Spiced Rum (see chapter 8, page 140)
½ cup dark rum

Put pineapple and papaya in large bowl. Sprinkle with coconut, then add cherries, mandarin orange slices, brown sugar, and lemon juice. Cover and let stand for 15 minutes. Add Vanilla Rum, Spiced Rum, and dark rum. Cover and refrigerate overnight. Store in refrigerator for up to 2 weeks.

YIELD: APPROX. 5 CUPS

Peaches in Amaretto

2 cups fresh, ripe peaches
1 tablespoon fruit protector
2 cups sugar
1 cup water
1 teaspoon lemon zest
1 teaspoon orange zest
¼ cup fresh-squeezed lemon juice
1 cup Almond Liqueur (see chapter 3, page 48)
½ cup 100-proof vodka
3 drops yellow food coloring
1 drop red food coloring

Peel peaches, cut in half, and remove pits. Immediately sprinkle with fruit protector to prevent browning. Bring sugar and water to a boil over medium-high heat, stirring constantly to prevent scorching. When clear, add peaches and continue cooking for 3 minutes more. Remove from heat and let cool for about 15 minutes. Transfer to clean 2-quart container. In small bowl, combine lemon zest, orange zest, lemon juice, Almond Liqueur, vodka, and yellow and red food coloring. Pour over peaches. If additional liquid is required to cover peaches, top off with simple syrup. Cover and let stand in a cool, dark place for at least 1 month before serving. YIELD: APPROX. 5 CUPS

Peach Marinade

Marinate pork tenderloin overnight in Peaches in Amaretto, then grill over hickory chips. Reduce the marinade over medium heat, add some chopped fresh sage, and use as a sauce over the grilled meat for a dish that is out of this world.

Double Raspberry Treat

If you love the flavor of raspberries, don't pass up this recipe. The liqueur makes an exciting addition to iced tea, and the fruits go great in fruit salad. If you are really into raspberries, serve the berries over raspberry sherbet and reduce some of the liqueur for a beautiful sauce.

> 2 cups fresh raspberries, picked and washed
> 1 cup sugar
> ½ cup water
> 1 teaspoon orange zest
> 1 tablespoon fresh-squeezed lemon juice
> 1 cup 100-proof vodka

Place raspberries in clean 1-quart container. Make a simple syrup by bringing sugar and water to a boil over medium-high heat, stirring constantly to prevent scorching. When clear, remove from heat and let stand until just warm. Stir in the orange zest, lemon juice, and vodka. Pour over raspberries. Let stand in a cool, dark place for at least 1 month before serving.

YIELD: APPROX. 1½ PINTS

CHAPTER 10

YOUR QUESTIONS ANSWERED

Q. How long can I keep the liqueurs I make?

A. Most of the liqueurs will keep indefinitely. Those with cream bases and those containing eggs should be stored in the refrigerator and used within one month.

Q. What should I do if I'm a little short of a full bottle?

A. Unlike wines, the quality of liqueurs isn't diminished by having bottles that aren't full. You also can store unused portions in the same bottle you serve from. If you want to make up full bottles, taste the liqueur. If you are satisfied with the balance of flavors, fill the bottle with one part base alcohol and two parts simple syrup.

Q. How do I alter recipes if I'm not really happy with my results?

A. Most liqueurs have three basic flavoring components: base alcohol, sweetener, and flavoring(s). You can alter any of these components to suit your taste. If one element is too strong, increase the proportion(s) of one or both of the others. If an element is not strong enough, add more (use simple syrup for a sweeter liqueur). Be sure to keep a record

157

of what you do so that you'll be able to duplicate it next time. If you make these adjustments, you usually do not need to age the liqueur as long as you did initially, but you might want to wait a week or two before serving.

Q. When I make coffee liqueurs, I notice that there is a thin film of oil on top. What causes it, and is it harmful to the liqueur?

A. The most likely cause is that you boiled the coffee. This oil can cause unwanted bitterness. The best cure is prevention: Don't boil your coffee. If you have used boiled coffee, strain the liqueur through cheesecloth dampened with water (so it doesn't absorb too much of the liqueur), and most of the oil should disappear.

Q. I've noticed that some of my nut liqueurs also have oil floating on top. Is this harmful to the liqueur?

A. Nuts contain a high percentage of oil, and alcohol extracts this oil. It is not harmful, but it may distract from the appearance of your liqueur. To remove the oil, first put the liqueur in the freezer for 2–3 hours or until the oil is partially solidified. Then rack or filter, leaving the surface oil behind, or use a small ladle to remove the oil, much as you would to remove congealed fat from soup stock.

Q. Sometimes when I use flavoring oils, the flavor is too strong for my taste. What can I do to reduce the flavor?

A. The best way to solve this problem is to place one teaspoon of flavoring oil in two tablespoons of 100-proof vodka or pure grain alcohol. Use this solution (which is known as an extract), one teaspoon at a time, to flavor your liqueur. Taste after each addition to achieve the intensity you want.

Q. Is it necessary to include the food coloring called for in some of the liqueur recipes?

A. Food coloring does not alter the flavor of the liqueur, but because people expect liqueurs to have intense colors, the absence of color may affect how the liqueur is perceived. Some liqueurs naturally have intense colors; others are essentially clear or amber until coloring agents are added. If you add color to your liqueurs, make sensible choices. Just as no one really wants to eat green mashed potatoes, most people don't want to drink liqueurs that violate their sense of what color a certain flavor should be.

Q. What's the best way to bottle my liqueurs?

A. You can keep your liqueurs in liquor bottles or glass jars, as long as the container has a tight-fitting lid so that the alcohol won't evaporate. If you plan to give your liqueurs as gifts, presentation is almost as important as the product. See page 15 for some suggestions.

Q. What is the best way to serve my liqueurs?

A. If you are going to serve your liqueurs by themselves, use your prettiest cordial glasses. Liqueurs are quite sweet and high in alcohol content, so a little goes a long way. If you're going to use your liqueurs in mixed drinks, choose a glass that's appropriate to the drink. Some liqueurs have a wonderful aroma. If you serve these in brandy snifters and warm them by holding them in your hand, you will enjoy both the flavor and the aroma of these cordials. Brandy snifters are especially nice for herb liqueurs, which have complex, sophisticated aromas. Liqueurs also are nice added to coffee or tea, either hot or iced. Finally, some liqueurs make elegant parfaits. We like to serve these "adult sundaes" in champagne glasses. Drizzle a little liqueur in the bottom of the glass, then layer it with ice cream.

SUPPLIERS

Sources for Flavorings

Belton, Inc.
2701 Thunderhawk Court
Dayton, OH 45414-0605
or
P.O. Box 13605
Dayton, OH 45413-0605
(937) 890-7768; 1-800-443-2266
Fax (937) 890-7780

The Brewtique
P.O. Box 723
Pine Grove, CA 95665
Phone or Fax (209) 296-5353
Online: brew@brewtique.com

Cellar Homebrew
14411 Greenwood Avenue N
Seattle, WA 98133
(206) 365-7660; Fax (206) 365-7677
Order line: 1-800-342-1871
e-mail: homebrew@aa.net

Davinci Gourmet
(206) 682-4682; (800)-640-6779

Entner-Stuart Premium Syrups
Corvallis, OR
(800) 377-9787; Fax (541) 758-0510

Folklore Foods, Inc.
Toppenish, WA
(509) 865-4772; Fax (509) 865-7363

Italia D'Oro
Portland, OR
(800) 545-4077; Fax (503) 669-2223

J W Crews & Company, Inc.
109 S. Georgia
P.O. Box 386
Troup, TX 75789
(903) 842-3327; (800) 707-8604
Fax (903) 842-2219
Online: info@crewscoffee.com

Lorann Oils
4518 Aurelius Rd.
P.O. Box 22009
Lansing, MI 48909-2009

Senza Rivale/Senza Zucchero
(800) 391-9649; Fax (206) 776-1375

Stearns & Lehman
Mansfield, OH
(800) 533-2722; Fax (419) 522-1152

Stirling Foods
Renton, WA
(800) 332-1714; Fax (206) 251-0251

Uptown Sales, Inc.
33 North Main Street
Chambersburg, PA 17201
(800) 548-9941

World Java House
(800) 528-3833
e-mail: http://www.worldjava.com/monin.htm

Converting Recipe Measurements to Metric

Use the following formulas for converting U.S. measurements to metric. Since the conversions are not exact, it's important to convert the measurements for all of the ingredients to maintain the same proportions as in the original recipe.

When the Measurement Given Is	Multiply It by	to Convert to
teaspoons	4.93	milliliters
tablespoons	14.79	milliliters
fluid ounces	29.57	milliliters
cups	236.59	milliliters
cups	0.236	liters
pints	473.18	milliliters
pints	0.473	liters
quarts	946.36	milliliters
quarts	0.946	liters
gallons	3.785	liters
ounces	28.35	grams
pounds	0.454	kilograms
inches	2.54	centimeters
degrees Fahrenheit	$\frac{5}{9}$ (temperature − 32)	degrees Celsius (Centigrade)

Glossary

AGING: Holding the cordial in a container for a month or so before serving to give the flavors time to interact and mellow. Although some of your cordials can be served as soon as the ingredients are mixed, they will have some rough edges if you do not allow the ingredients to "get to know one another."

ALCOHOL: Ethyl alcohol is the component in cordials that acts as a preservative and as an intoxicant. Cordials are usually served in very small glasses. They taste delicious, but don't forget that too much of these, as with other alcoholic beverages, can make you incapable of driving and operating machinery.

ARTIFICIAL SWEETENER: A substance such as saccharine or aspartame that imparts sweetness without using sugars. We do not recommend using artificial sweeteners in cordials.

BALANCE: Achieved when the alcohol content, sweetener, and flavoring components are complementary. Cordials are said to be balanced when these elements harmonize.

BODY: The texture or "mouth feel" of the liqueur. Traditionally, cordials are thicker than other alcoholic beverages. The body of cordials is often achieved by adding glycerin. Glycerin does not affect the flavor of the cordial. If you prefer a "thinner" beverage, you may omit the glycerin from the recipes that call for it.

CLARIFYING: The process by which suspended particles in cordials are removed. Clarifying is usually achieved by racking, filtering, or straining the cordials.

CORDIAL: In the United States, an alcoholic beverage with a high sugar content, an alcohol base, and a variety of flavorings. In Europe, such beverages are usually called liqueurs.

CORN SYRUP: A sweetener derived from corn, often used to sweeten soft drinks and cordials.

CREAM-BASED LIQUEUR: A liqueur that contains milk or cream, or sometimes finely pureed coconut. Unlike other liqueurs, cream-based liqueurs should be refrigerated.

DISTILLATION: A process that concentrates alcohol by heating it in a solution and then cooling the vapors. Distillation of alcoholic beverages at home is illegal. When you create cordials at home, you will use distilled liquors, the taxes for which have already been paid by the distiller.

ESSENCE: A flavoring component in which a concentrated flavoring agent, such as orange oil, is dissolved in a high-proof alcohol base.

EXTRACT: A flavoring component with an alcohol base, such as vanilla extract.

FLAVORING OIL: A flavoring component with an oil base, such as walnut flavoring oil.

GLYCERIN: A sweet amino acid, usually derived from sugarcane, that gives some cordials their characteristic body.

LIQUOR: A general term for alcoholic beverages created by the process of distillation, which includes such things as whiskey, rum, vodka, brandy, gin, and so on.

LIQUEUR: See *cordial*.

PROOF: A term used to describe the alcohol content of wines and spirits. It is equal to twice the percentage of alcohol in a solution. A liquor with a 40 percent concentration of alcohol, then, is an 80-proof liquor.

RACKING: The name given to the process of siphoning cleared cordials from a holding vessel into a clean container. Racking removes the clarified cordial and leaves fruit solids, impurities, and other residue behind.

SIMPLE SYRUP: A syrup made by mixing sugar and water and heating it until the sugar dissolves into solution. Many of the cordial recipes in this book call for simple syrup because home cordial makers sometimes find it difficult to dissolve sugars in alcohol bases.

SUGAR: Any of a variety of sweeteners that may be used to give cordials their characteristic sweetness, such as fructose (fruit sugars), sucrose (table sugar derived from sugar beets or sugarcane), or corn syrup.

ZEST: The outer rind of citrus fruits, which is rich in concentrated flavoring oils. Zest may be removed with a zester or vegetable peeler. Be sure to use only the colored portion of the rind and not the white inner peel when preparing zests for your liqueurs; the white inner peel eventually makes the cordials bitter.

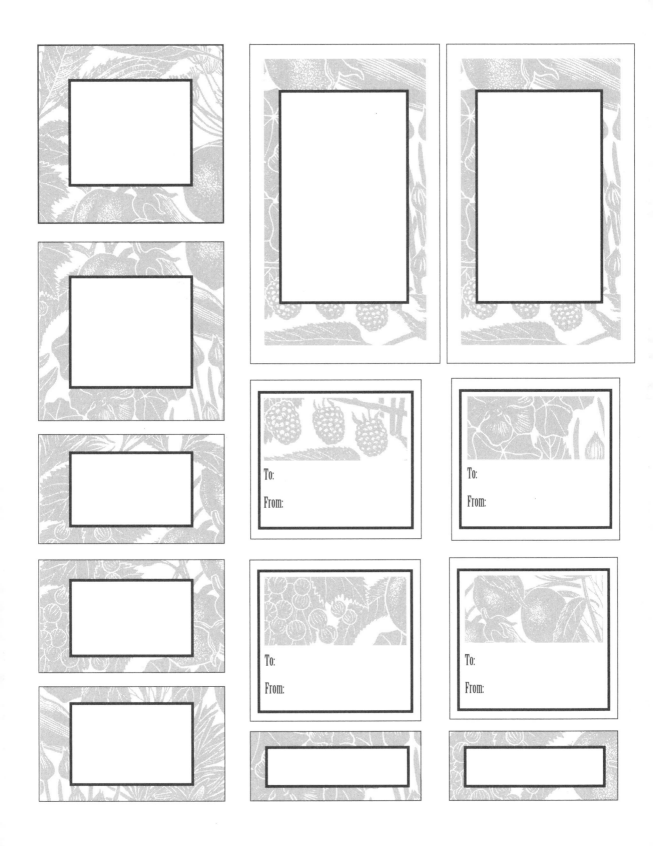

To:

From:

To:

From:

To:

From:

To:

From:

INDEX

OTHER STOREY TITLES
YOU WILL ENJOY

Herbed Wine Cuisine, by Janice Mancuso. Unique techniques for flavoring store-bought or home-made wine with herbs, flowers, fruits, and spices. Includes more than 100 easy-to-make recipes using the wines, many of which are low-fat or fat-free, and use little or no salt. 160 pages. Hard-cover. ISBN 0-88266-967-2.

Country Wines, by Pattie Vargas and Rich Gulling. How to make delicious wines from fruits and berries, flowers, and herbs. 176 pages. Paperback. ISBN 0-88266-749-1.

Herbal Vinegar, by Maggie Oster. Dozens of ideas for making and flavoring spice, vegetable, and flower vinegars, including more than 100 recipes for cooking with flavored recipes. Also contains hints and instructions for more than 100 vinegar-based personal and household uses. 176 pages. Paperback. ISBN 0-88266-843-9.

Herb Mixtures & Spicy Blends, edited by Deborah Balmuth. An essential guide to dozens of easy-to-make recipes — the favorites of herb growers and sellers across the United States — that use herb mixtures and spice blends to create healthy, tasty dishes without a lot of added salt or fat. 160 pages. Paperback. ISBN 0-88266-918-4.

From Vines to Wines: The Complete Guide to Growing Grapes and Making Your Own Wine, by Jeff Cox. A guide to the entire winemaking process, from evaluating the vineyard site and choosing the best grape species to bottling, supplies, and troubleshooting. 288 pages. Paperback. ISBN 0-88266-528-6.

These books and other Storey books are available at your bookstore, farm store, garden center, or directly from Storey Publishing, Schoolhouse Road, Pownal, Vermont 05261, or by calling 1-800-441-5700. WWW.STOREY.COM